Let's Take
LONDON

D0882062

David Stewart White
Deb Hosey White

Castlerigg Press

© 2018 by David Stewart White and Deb Hosey White

All rights reserved

6th edition

ISBN 978-1-7322706-0-2

For more information about family travel to London, please visit the website at:

www.KidsToLondon.com

My Dad says that being a Londoner has nothing to do with where you're born. He says that there are people who get off a jumbo jet at Heathrow, go through immigration waving any kind of passport, hop on the tube and by the time the train's pulled into Piccadilly Circus they've become a Londoner.

— *Moon Over Soho* by Ben Aaronovitch

London is so vast and varied, so rich in what is interesting, that to one who would wander among its treasures, it can be difficult to decide where to begin, and even more difficult to decide where to end. Indeed, to a book on London—to a thousand books on London—there is no end.

—*A Wander in London* by E. V. Lucas

Contents

Acknowledgments

Our thanks to the many people on both sides of the pond who have assisted us along the way to this edition of *Let's Take the Kids to London*. A nod to our children, Dan and Laura, whose travel adventures and encouragement helped launch this book.

A special word of appreciation to the skilled photographers whose works appear through Creative Commons licenses and other arrangements. There are some very talented people taking photographs around the world and many of them are generous enough to share their pictures with the rest of us.

London Loves Kids

London is one of the world's most family friendly cities. With open arms, it welcomes kids to explore and make their own memories. Look around London and you notice children of all ages playing in parks, romping through fantastic playgrounds, skipping along the Thames Path to ride the London Eye, investigating hands-on museums, and soaking up history as they explore famous landmarks. The landscape of London invites children to look, listen, laugh, and learn.

London loves kids. You will know it's true when you see a yeoman warder at the Tower of London bending down to listen to a child's question. Or you watch a teenaged tourist trying to elicit a smile from a stone-faced palace guard. Or you notice a museum guide quietly leading a child to the front of the group for the best view.

London and kids are made for each other. The city has long been the adopted home of Paddington Bear, and Peter Pan moved into Kensington Gardens ages ago. Harry Potter and his friends have been catching the train to Hogwarts from King's Cross Station for quite a few years now. Long ago, Mary Poppins landed in town and worked as a nanny. And Christopher Robin first met a bear named Pooh in the London Zoo before moving to the Hundred Acre Wood.

There is a reason why the title of this book is *Let's Take the Kids to London*. That's exactly what we said when our family of four took its first, serendipitous trip to Britain. From that experience, the trips that followed, and many years of ongoing research, we converted the phrase into this book.

So fix a cup of tea, sit back, prop up your feet and read. Initial planning for a trip is a time for dreaming. We will paint a picture of London; you can imagine your family in the picture. We start with the prime tourist destinations in central London. After that, we explore up and down the River Thames. Next, we cover family activities in and around London. Then we provide some ideas for field trips to give you a taste of what lies outside London in the English countryside. Finally, it's down to practical matters with some planning advice and travel tips we have learned along the way.

London Landmarks

Towers and Bridges

Much of London's history is locked behind the imposing walls of the Tower of London. William Wallace, Anne Boleyn, Thomas Cromwell, and Catherine Howard were all temporary Tower residents. And, unlike the unfortunate prisoners who left the Tower without their heads, today's visitors can walk out the gates and tour another nearby landmark—Tower Bridge.

The Tower of London

"I know where we're going," said Judy, as they turned a corner.

"It's the Tower of London!" exclaimed Jonathan.

Paddington had never been to the Tower of London before and he was most impressed. It was much, much bigger than he had pictured.

— *Paddington at the Tower* by Michael Bond and Fred Banbery

Will kids enjoy the Tower of London? Absolutely! In fact, if you have time to take your children to only one historic spot in London, make it the Tower. The Tower of London offers a virtual smorgasbord of English history and culture within its ancient walls. Take your pick from this partial menu:

- Beauty—the crown jewels
- Tragedy—dismal dungeons and prison cells galore
- Legend—captive ravens and wandering ghosts
- Horror—beheadings on Tower Green
- Tradition—the ancient Ceremony of the Keys

The Tower's yeoman warder tour guides are informative and friendly, and most make a special effort to pique the interests of young visitors. A tour with a yeoman warder may be the "crown jewel" of a Tower visit because the warders provide an insider's perspective that is every bit as memorable as the real crown jewels displayed in the Tower.

Please don't call them beefeaters. These are yeoman warders, retired career members of the British military. The Tower of London is home to many of the thirty-seven warders who live with their families on the grounds. Look closely and you may spot the domestic mixed in with the historic—children's play equipment, a pet cat, hanging laundry, and other evidence of the residents' private lives. The Tower forms a walled village within the city of London, but the private pub and staff housing are not on the public tour.

One stop on the Tower tour where visitors may get a sense of this community is the Chapel of St. Peter ad Vincula. Although this is a royal chapel and historic site, it is also the local church for Tower

residents. The royal family worships here on occasion, and this is also where yeoman warders' grandchildren may be baptized.

William the Conqueror began building the Tower in 1078, shortly after taking over England. Constructing the imposing Tower was his way of letting the natives know that London was under new management. The Tower was expanded over hundreds of years to become the fortress you see today. It has served as prison, palace, zoo, armory, execution spot, place of worship, and tourist attraction.

The beautiful crown jewels are one of the Tower's most popular exhibits. A moving walkway inches visitors past the jewel cases to ensure that everyone has an unobstructed view, but no one lingers too long. If it is not too crowded, you can usually circle back for another look.

Children may find the security precautions in the Jewel House almost as impressive as the jewels themselves. The massive doors leave no doubt that you are walking through a very large vault to view the jewels. The high-tech, high-security Jewel House is a far cry from the original display of jewels in the Tower. In the seventeenth century, the crown jewels were simply locked in a cabinet. When visitors wanted to see the jewels, they just asked a custodian and paid a small fee! Not surprisingly, someone attempted to steal the jewels, but the thieves were caught making their getaway. Security was tightened, repeatedly, and the jewels have been safely guarded ever since.

The White Tower contains displays of ancient armor and weapons including Tudor and Stuart royal armor, weapons from the reign of Henry VIII, and British war trophies. Kids will be drawn to the child-sized armor worn by young princes and to the equine armor that protected royal horses.

Tower Green was the site of several notorious executions. King Henry VIII had a frequent-chopper account here. Two of his wives—Anne Boleyn and Catherine Howard—were executed on the green after being imprisoned in the Tower. Queen Jane Grey was also beheaded in the Tower, and all three unfortunate ladies are buried in the Chapel of St. Peter ad Vincula.

But for all its association with beheadings and imprisonment, today's Tower does not feel very macabre. Leave that to tourist traps in the city like the London Dungeon or Clink Museum. The Tower's yeoman warders may spin a few sinister stories of executions that elicit "eews" and "yucks" from the audience, but the warders are so good-natured that a visit to the Tower is appropriate for all ages.

Sir Walter Raleigh was one famous Tower prisoner familiar to many American visitors. Imprisoned here three times, Sir Walter made himself quite comfortable in the Tower. His family moved in with him and brought along furniture, books, and other homey touches. But— and this is a big "but"—Sir Walter was executed after his third stay in the Tower. He lost his head elsewhere in London, not on Tower Green.

Today the Tower's only prisoners are a flock of birds. Visitors will undoubtedly hear the legend: if the ravens leave the Tower of London, the town is toast! Actually, that's not exactly the legend, but it does explain why the birds' wings are clipped. The legend really says that if the ravens leave, the White Tower will crumble and disaster will befall England.

The national importance of the ravens was demonstrated during an unfortunate incident at the Tower of London. In preparation for a visit by the royal family, a police dog sniffed through the Tower grounds searching for possible bombs. During the search, Charlie the bomb dog was pecked by Charlie the raven. A former bird-hunter, canine Charlie grabbed raven Charlie in his mouth. The raven  struggled and the dog instinctively bit down, killing the bird. The British press had a field day, members of the public were outraged, and the dog was demoted. But the yeoman warder who told us most of this story was nonplussed: "Not a big deal. We can always get another raven."

Canine threats are an ongoing concern for the yeoman warder responsible for the birds. The Tower's Raven Master locks the ravens into protective cages each night, in part because of London's burgeoning urban fox population.

During the summer months thousands of tourists stream into the Tower of London. Plan to arrive as soon as it opens and head straight for the crown jewels to avoid the long lines found later in the day. You can buy a ticket in advance on the Tower's website, in a few London Underground stations, and from some tour operators.

The Ceremony of the Keys

Want to see a free and nearly private ceremony in the Tower of London? The Tower allows about fifty people to attend the nightly Ceremony of the Keys—the ancient ceremonial locking of the Tower gates. Attending the ceremony requires advance planning. Tickets may be ordered from the Tower's website (search under "Ceremony of the Keys"). Tickets are free except for a small administrative fee. Tickets are limited and extremely popular, so book as far in advance as possible—nine months to a year ahead is best. Photo identification is required when entering the ceremony, and children under eighteen must be accompanied by an adult.

On the night of the ceremony, ticket holders are escorted into the Tower at 9:30 p.m., long after other visitors have left. A yeoman warder explains the history of the solemn seven-hundred-year-old ceremonial locking of the Tower's gates. After a brief introduction, visitors line up near the Bloody Tower gate to watch the Tower of London's military guard unit escort the chief warder as he locks the Tower. Today, the Ceremony of the Keys is largely symbolic, but to understand how important this ceremony is, consider our family's experience.

A huge celebration was taking place at nearby Tower Bridge. A band was playing outside the Tower of London's walls, but arrangements had been made to stop the music during the Ceremony of the Keys, which has been going on every night for hundreds of years without interruption. Visitors gathered inside the Tower at the appointed hour. The guards were ready to begin the ceremony, but the band outside kept playing. The yeoman warder looked at his watch, frowned, and looked again—but still there was no break in the music. At this point the warder's supervisor appeared, barked a command into his radio and made a pointed comment about "putting an end to this nonsense." He ran off, and a minute or so later the band abruptly stopped mid-song. Maybe it was coincidence, or maybe the bandleader was reminded of the many executions carried out just a few hundred feet away. In any case, the Ceremony of the Keys began without musical interruptions.

On another visit to the Tower of London, we learned that it's not just the yeoman warders who take the ceremony seriously. Different British military units rotate guard duty at the Tower. On this visit, the guards were Gurkhas, elite British Army troops from Nepal. During the ceremony, the guards' commands were issued in crisp, loud, and heavily accented English. It was the same ceremony as performed by regular British troops, but visitors almost needed subtitles to understand it. After the ceremony, a yeoman warder explained that the Gurkhas take guarding the Tower very seriously and very literally. The standing order for the guard is that all visitors have to leave the Tower immediately after attending a chapel service. One Christmas Eve the Gurkha guards escorted all churchgoers out of the Tower— no exceptions—including family members of yeoman warders who live inside the Tower's grounds. The exiled family members had to phone friends inside the Tower to get back into their own homes. The Gurkha guards certainly secured the Tower, but you wonder if they allowed Santa Claus in that night.

Here are a few practical hints for visitors attending the Ceremony of the Keys. Arrive early. If possible, stay in the front of the tour group and stand directly opposite the gate to the Bloody Tower. When signaled by the yeoman warder, move quickly through the gate to see the completion of the ceremony in the inner courtyard. The yeoman warders ask that visitors not talk during the ceremony. Silence is more than a mark of respect. Half the fun of the ceremony is listening to the sounds—the guards' synchronous footsteps on the cobblestones, the jangling keys, the shouted commands, the bugler's notes. One other important fact, especially for visitors with children, is that the Tower's restroom facilities are not open immediately before, during, or after the Ceremony of the Keys. The following is a true story; the names have been omitted to protect the easily embarrassed.

Hearing the first footfalls of the guards, the father peered down the pathway toward the gate of the Byward Tower. "Dad. Dad!" whispered a small, urgent voice. "I have to go to the bathroom." Hoping against the inevitable, the father replied, "Can't you wait, son? The bathrooms are all closed." But alas, as every parent knows, when a child has to go, he has to go, even in the Tower of London. Fortunately, a sympathetic yeoman warder stepped in, earning the father's enduring gratitude. "Bring the little fellow this way," he offered, and led the pair through a gate toward the White Tower. "Let him use the wall. It's seen worse," said the ever-practical warder. The crisis was resolved, but the father and son missed the start of the ceremony. We have it on good authority that they returned to the Tower the following year to see the entire Ceremony of the Keys. This time, they planned ahead and used the public toilets at Tower Place just outside the Tower gates.

Tower Chapel Services and Special Events

Toilet emergencies aside, there is another way to see more of the Tower than the average tourist. If you are truly interested, ask a yeoman warder about attending Sunday church services in the Tower's Chapel Royal of St. Peter ad Vincula. Remember, this is not a tourist event. It is a worship service for people who live in the Tower. Go with respect.

Special events abound at the Tower, particularly on weekends in the summer, during school breaks, and around major holidays. It is a good idea to check the Historic Royal Palaces website for information on upcoming events. One event that is hard to ignore is a gun salute. For royal occasions such as the monarch's birthday, a simple twenty-one-gun salute just won't do. The Tower fires off a sixty-two-gun salute: the traditional twenty-one-gun salute, plus twenty because the Tower is a royal palace and fortress, and twenty-one more as a mark of respect for the sovereign. Since the end of World War II, the Honourable Artillery Company (the oldest armed body in Britain) has fired gun salutes from four modern cannons on Tower Wharf.

With buildings and fortifications that are almost one thousand years old, archeological and restoration work is an ongoing endeavor at the Tower of London. Some of these projects unearth "new" information about the Tower's history. This makes the Tower more than a static historical site—it is living history.

If you plan to visit the Tower, Hampton Court, and at least one other Historic Royal Palaces property, consider purchasing an annual membership. Getting tickets in advance will let you avoid waiting in long lines. Buy tickets on the Tower's website, by phone, from a London Underground Travel Information Centre, or at the Tower ticket office.

There is a restaurant and snack kiosk inside the Tower grounds and more restaurants, fast food and other options can be found just outside. There are no formal outdoor picnic areas, but visitors may bring food and sit on benches on the Tower's grounds. There are toilets and baby changing areas in the Tower's restaurant and several other locations. Many areas of the Tower are not wheelchair or stroller accessible.

Website: www.hrp.org.uk

Tower Bridge

Tower Bridge rivals Big Ben as the most recognizable landmark in London. Don't make the tourist's mistake of referring to Tower Bridge as London Bridge. Despite the famous children's song, London Bridge is not falling down. It is a sturdy modern bridge upstream on the River Thames. Its predecessor was sold, dismantled, and reassembled as a tourist attraction in Lake Havasu, Arizona. Today's London Bridge is hardly a tourist attraction, but Tower Bridge deserves a visit.

Take a tour of the inner workings of Tower Bridge and learn how the span was opened in Victorian times by huge steam engines. Kids can experiment with operating models and interactive displays that detail the drawbridge's engineering principles. Technically, Tower Bridge is a *bascule* bridge, from the French word for seesaw. Undoubtedly this is the largest seesaw in London. Once outside the engine rooms, take in the views from the top of the bridge, 140 feet above. There is an enclosed walkway with clear glass floors—great views of the traffic below and the nearby riverside.

If you want to forgo the museum and enclosed walkway, there is no charge to stroll across the bridge on the road-level sidewalk. This is a great place to take a picture of the family, so set up the shot to include the Tower of London in the background. Lucky visitors may see the bridge being raised to let a ship go past. Bridge openings are rare these days because London is no longer the port that it once was. But there is no shortage of traffic on the bridge; nearly 40,000 cars, trucks, and buses cross this important London link every day.

Ticket prices to the exhibit are moderate and there are discounts for families, students, and seniors. Children under age five get in free. Tickets can be purchased at the bridge or online. There are toilets and baby changing areas onsite and the bridge is wheelchair accessible.

Website: www.towerbridge.org.uk

Palaces and Horses

Royal residences, royal horses, and royal treasures are all parts of London's history. Although today's monarchy is mainly ceremonial, the trappings of royalty still serve important roles... as tourist attractions.

Buckingham Palace

> "By gumdrops!" whispered the Big
> Friendly Giant. "Is this really it?"
>
> "There's the Palace," Sophie whispered back.
>
> Not more than a hundred yards away, through the tall
> trees in the garden, across the mown lawn and the
> tidy flowerbeds, the massive shape of the Palace itself
> loomed through the darkness. It was made of whitish
> stone. The sheer size of it staggered the BFG.
>
> —*The BFG* by Roald Dahl

The Big Friendly Giant had good reason to be impressed. A 2017 report on the world's most expensive houses ranked Buckingham Palace as number one, with a value of almost US $1.6 billion. The grandeur of Buckingham Palace doesn't come strictly from architecture but from its aura of tradition, ceremony, and power.

The royal family allows the public to peek inside Buckingham Palace. Just a peek mind you, and only for a few weeks each year while the royals are on vacation. Under this arrangement, Buckingham Palace state rooms are usually open daily during August and September. Tourists are admitted at timed intervals, the lines can be long and security is tight. Audio tours are provided, including a family audio tour to help

kids enjoy their visit. Pick up a children's garden activity trail map, too.

Seeing the inside of Buckingham Palace is not just a novelty for foreign tourists. A fair number of British citizens take the tour to check out the inside of a place that has played an important, if ceremonial, role in their nation's history. During one August visit, we overheard a British mother telling her two daughters, "This is the piano where the young princesses Elizabeth and Margaret took their lessons when they were little girls." We will never know if this fact was impressive enough to inspire the visiting children to practice their piano lessons, but the mother deserves credit for trying. Another visiting child was unimpressed by the Buckingham Palace throne room. "That's the throne? It's just an old red chair!"

At the end of the Buckingham Place tour you can stroll through parts of the palace's thirty-nine-acre private garden. As the tour ends, there is an opportunity to browse the palace gift shop, filled with tasteful but expensive mementos of the visit.

The palace sometimes offers tours on select dates in December, January, and February. Complete with an end-of-tour glass of champagne and a ticket price to match, these guided tours are not

geared to family groups. The rest of the year, tourists are reduced to gawking at Buckingham Palace through a tall iron fence. Invariably someone (usually a child) asks, "Is anybody home?" For an answer, take a look at the roof. If the royal standard has been raised —the flag with a lion on it—the monarch is in residence. The British Union Jack flies at Buckingham when the royals are away from home.

By the way, when you peer through the fence, you're actually looking at the back of Buckingham Palace. The front of the palace overlooks the private gardens.

Parts of the palace are not wheelchair accessible. Strollers (pushchairs) and large packages must be checked at the entrance. Families may borrow baby carriers for use during the palace tour. Toilets are available at the end of the tour.

Websites: www.royal.gov.uk
www.royalcollection.org.uk

Several nearby tourist sites are associated with Buckingham Palace:
- The Royal Mews
- Clarence House
- Wellington Arch
- The Queen's Gallery

For a slightly better peek into the royal backyard, climb to the top of nearby Wellington Arch. Spying on the palace grounds will entice many children, but the Queen's Gallery art collection and Clarence House may be of limited interest to kids. The Royal Mews, site of the palace's stables and carriage house, is another matter.

Horse Feathers? The Royal Mews

Why would a horse stable be called a mews? Originally, this was the home of the royal falcons, and mewing referred to the shedding of the birds' feathers. Today the Mews is the headquarters of the Crown Equerry—the motor pool for the royal family. This is where the royal family's ceremonial coaches, limos, and horses are housed.

The royals own more than one hundred coaches and carriages; some of the most ornate are on display in the Royal Mews. For sheer opulence, check out the Gold State Coach. As the name implies, this coach is so heavily gilded it's a wonder that the royal horses can even pull it. The golden fairy-tale coach has been used at every coronation since 1821. Slightly lower on the opulence scale is the Irish State Coach, used at the annual opening of Parliament, and the Glass Coach, which transported Lady Diana Spencer to St. Paul's Cathedral to begin her star-crossed marriage to Prince Charles. For the 2011 wedding

of Prince William to Kate Middleton, the newlyweds traveled from Westminster Abbey back to Buckingham Palace riding in a vintage carriage built in 1902 for the coronation of King Edward VII.

Children touring the Royal Mews may quickly conclude that once they've seen one golden coach, they've seen them all. Let's see the horses! The royal family lives in luxury at Buckingham Palace, so it is no surprise that the royal horses' quarters are pretty fancy too. It doesn't even smell like a stable. The Cleveland Bay and Windsor Grey horses live in clean, bright stalls with tiled walls and each animal's name displayed on a prominent placard. The Royal Mews is also home to a fleet of automobiles. But the official in charge of the Mews has the title Master of the Queen's Horses, not Master of the Queen's Rolls-Royces. It is horses and carriages that most tourists come to see. The Mews is an agreeable attraction for most children, and for young equestrians the Mews is a must-see.

The Mews features a learning room where kids can imagine, draw, and color their own royal carriages. Toilets and baby changing areas are available at the Mews and the site is wheelchair accessible.

Website: www.royalcollection.org.uk

Clarence House

No one lives forever, but before her death at age 101, Elizabeth, the Queen Mother, was truly pushing the longevity envelope. Clarence House was her home for almost half a century, from 1953 to 2002. After she died, Prince Charles moved into Clarence House and did a bit of redecorating, but he kept much of the house the way his grandmother left it.

Clarence House was designed by John Nash, the same architect largely responsible for Buckingham Palace, Regent's Park, Marble Arch, and a host of other Regency-style structures in London. Clarence House was built in 1827, and the site was heavily damaged in World War II. Like Buckingham Palace, Clarence House is open to the public during the summer. Clarence House is not a grand palace and the tour includes just a handful of official rooms on the ground floor of the building. There is little to interest children here on the forty-five minute guided tour.

There are no toilets available onsite. The house tour is wheelchair accessible. Strollers and large packages must be checked at the entrance.

Website: www.royalcollection.org.uk

Wellington Arch

Except for the summer opening, the gates to Buckingham Palace are generally closed to the public. But tourists can always sneak a peek of the palace grounds from Wellington Arch near Hyde Park Corner. Visitors climb steps or take the elevator to the top of the arch and peer into the palace gardens and tennis courts.

Wellington Arch was once an entryway into Buckingham Palace. The arch was built to celebrate the victory of the Duke of Wellington over Napoleon Bonaparte. At one time, the arch sported a huge equestrian statue of the duke. That monstrosity was removed and the arch was relocated in the late 1800s. Now the arch supports the largest bronze sculpture in Europe—an angel of peace landing atop a horse-drawn chariot of war.

Until the 1950s the arch housed London's smallest police station. The Wellington Arch was restored by the English Heritage preservation organization and opened to the public. English Heritage also operates nearby Apsley House, home of the Duke of Wellington.

There are no food or toilet facilities in Wellington Arch, but most of the site is wheelchair accessible.

Website: www.english-heritage.org.uk

The Queen's Gallery

On September 13, 1940, German bombs hit Buckingham Palace. King George IV and Queen Elizabeth escaped unharmed, but the royal chapel was not so lucky—it was demolished. In 1962, after languishing for years, the ruined chapel was converted to a gallery exhibiting items from the monarch's art collection.

When Buckingham Palace is not open, a visit to the Queen's Gallery provides the flavor of the palace through an extensive display of royal artwork and furnishings. For a child, visiting the Queen's Gallery could be a test of patience. But you can borrow activity bags to take on your family tour of the gallery. And on weekends and holidays the gallery livens things up with family workshops and activities for kids.

There is no food in the gallery, but toilets and baby changing rooms are available and the site is wheelchair accessible. Backpacks and large packages must be checked at the entrance.

Website: www.royalcollection.org.uk

Old Dead Guys

Touring cathedrals and churches may not rank high on your children's sightseeing priority lists. But if there is one ancient church in London for a family to see, it is Westminster Abbey. Or maybe St. Paul's Cathedral. Westminster Abbey is a fascinating site, drenched in history—and the same can be said for St. Paul's Cathedral. One or both deserve a spot on your itinerary.

Westminster Abbey

We read about kings and queens in history books. But that's not the same as visiting their final resting places. In Westminster Abbey you will find the tombs of Henry III, Henry V, Queen Elizabeth I, and Mary Queen of Scots, as well as 3,300 other people! The roll call includes

such famous names as David Livingston, Isaac Newton, Charles Darwin, George Frederic Handel, Laurence Olivier and Stephen Hawking. At least one person, poet Ben Jonson, was buried standing upright. The infamous Oliver Cromwell was only a temporary abbey resident. Cromwell's body was removed by royal decree in the mid-1600s. The oldest of the interred was Thomas Parr, whose improbable claim to fame was that he lived for more than 152 years before being buried in the abbey in 1635.

Will so many "old dead guys" grab a child's interest? Not all of Westminster Abbey's history is ancient. Queen Elizabeth II was crowned here in 1953, and the abbey was the site of Princess Diana's funeral in 1997, the Queen Mother's funeral in 2002, and the wedding of Prince William and Kate Middleton in 2011. The abbey was also the location for a bit of action in *The Da Vinci Code*. The popular novel includes scenes featuring Sir Isaac Newton's tomb and the Chapter House in Westminster Abbey, but The Da Vinci Code movie was not filmed here. Westminster Abbey officials took a dim theological view of the story and denied entry to the filmmakers. The abbey is truly camera shy—refusing offers to appear in *The King's Speech* and the BBC adaptation of *King Charles III*.

Although not its most glorious moment in modern history, the abbey got a nod in an episode of The Simpsons when Homer and Bart undertook the challenge of building a model of the elaborate landmark. Quipped Homer, "All we have to do is follow the directions." Recent history aside, Westminster Abbey is *old*. One of the first things William the Conqueror did after taking over England was to have himself crowned in the Norman abbey that stood on the site

of Westminster Abbey. That was in 1066, more than 900 years ago. Westminster Abbey was rebuilt in 1245.

But again, is so much ancient history going to turn young visitors into enthusiastic tourists? One option is to pick up a copy of A Children's Trail—a free guidebook for kids available at the abbey's information desk. There are other ways to help prevent kids' eyes from glazing over while touring the abbey. Tell them to look up as they enter Henry VII's Lady Chapel, and they will find the banners and crests of the knights of the Order of the Bath (the *clean* knights). If it isn't too crowded, this is a good opportunity to take a moment, sit down, and study the variety of knights' shields and colorful banners, which incorporate a menagerie of animals, weaponry, and peculiar symbols. Kids can pick out favorites and speculate about some of the more unusual shields. Ask children what their shields would look like if they became knights of the Order of the Bath.

There are some newer additions to Westminster Abbey. Two stained glass windows were installed in the Lady Chapel in 2013. The glass commemorates the sixtieth anniversary of Queen Elizabeth II's coronation. Another modern historical tidbit that kids can search for in Westminster Abbey is a tiny hole in the wall at the back of the Lady Chapel. The hole was blasted out during the bombing of London in World War II. It is near a memorial dedicated to Royal Air Force members who fought in the Battle of Britain. The tiny hole was the only appreciable war damage to the abbey, despite being situated just a block from the tempting targets of Parliament and other government buildings. The Royal Air Force chapel window includes the crests from sixty-eight fighter squadrons that fought in the Battle of Britain in 1940.

Turn your attention to more old dead guys at Poet's Corner in the south transept of the abbey. Some kids may recognize the poets, writers, and actors buried and memorialized in Poet's Corner. This impressive Dead Poets' Society includes Geoffrey Chaucer, Charles Dickens, Alfred Lord Tennyson, Robert Browning, and Rudyard Kipling.

Westminster Abbey's "attic"—the medieval triforium—has been converted into a new museum and gallery. The Queen's Diamond

Jubilee Galleries, located seventy feet above the Abbey floor, display treasures that were once hidden away in storage areas. The views from the attic are pretty amazing too.

Next stop is the cloisters, a covered square of corridors once used by the abbey's monks and now filled with memorial plaques. The nearby Chapter House was the site of Parliament meetings in the fourteenth century. The College Garden is worth a look, although its hours differ from the Abbey's. During summer months, lunchtime concerts are sometimes held in the garden. The abbey's museum also deserves a visit, if time and attention spans allow. Kids can dress up as monks in the museum.

Not every monument or hidden mystery in Westminster Abbey is ancient or even mysterious. Observant visitors to the abbey grounds can find one monument many guidebooks ignore. Thomas Crapper—the memorably named plumber—was employed here in the late 1800s to install plumbing fixtures. Several manhole covers bearing the inscription T. CRAPPER & CO. remain today around Westminster Abbey.

Westminster Abbey is so overrun with milling tourists that it can be difficult to hold religious services. Remember, you are visiting a historic site and an active church where people come to worship and pray.

One final note. Despite its size, Westminster Abbey is not a cathedral; it is a "royal peculiar." The term means that the abbey reports to the British monarch instead of to the normal church hierarchy of bishops and archbishops. Technically, the abbey is named the Collegiate Church of St. Peter, Westminster, but don't try asking directions using that official moniker. Of course, it's no longer really an abbey because there are no monks in residence, but there once were, and the name remains.

You can grab a meal in the Cellarium Café, located in the cellars where the abbey's monks once stored their food and drink (menus have been updated since the fourteenth century). There is also a snack kiosk outside the west entrance. Toilets are located in the café and in the abbey's cloisters. Some areas of the abbey are not wheelchair accessible.

Website: www.westminster-abbey.org

St. Paul's Cathedral

> But at last they came to St. Paul's Cathedral, which was built a long time ago by a man with a bird's name. Wren it was... That is why so many birds live near Sir Christopher Wren's Cathedral, which also belongs to St. Paul, and that is why the Bird Woman lives there, too.
>
> —*Mary Poppins* by P. L. Travers

The original St. Paul's burned down during the Great Fire of London in 1666, so the current cathedral is a relative newcomer compared to Westminster Abbey. Visiting children may note one effect of this newness: the old dead guys buried in St. Paul's are not as old, numerous, or famous as those buried in Westminster Abbey. They are just as dead, however. At this point in the narrative, we offer a blanket

apology to the deceased and to any readers who are offended. In our defense, please remember that this is a book about kids as tourists, and "old dead guys" is a realistic child's-eye view of touring cathedrals and churches.

St. Paul's is a fitting monument to Sir Christopher Wren, London's greatest architect. Wren is buried here—yikes, another old dead guy!—with the simple inscription *Si monumentum requiris circumspice.* In case your Latin is rusty, we'll translate: "If you seek a monument, look around you." Other notables buried in St. Paul's are the Duke of Wellington and Admiral Lord Nelson. Gross-out note for kids: Nelson died at the Battle of Trafalgar in 1805, and his body was placed in a keg of brandy for the long trip home. Good plan, but the sailors allegedly drank all the brandy before they returned to home port!

One fascinating feature of the cathedral is the Whispering Gallery. It is a long climb to reach the gallery high inside the dome above the cathedral floor. After you catch your breath, turn and whisper against the circular wall. Your words can be heard on the other side of the dome, almost 130 feet away. While in the gallery take a look at the cathedral's frescoes. Climb even higher to reach the Golden Gallery.

This is a fantastic observation point from which to see the entire city of London, but the climb is long and dizzying, with almost 200 steps to the Whispering Gallery and a narrow 500 steps to the very top.

American visitors may be particularly interested in the American Memorial Chapel located behind the high altar. This is a British tribute to 28,000 Americans based in Britain who lost their lives during World War II. A book containing the names of the war dead is displayed in the chapel.

Christopher Wren wanted to rebuild the entire city of London after the Great Fire of 1666. He had even grander plans for St. Paul's Cathedral. It was not enough that the 360-foot-high dome dominated the London skyline. Wren wanted the dome to be gilded. Budget concerns nixed the gold plating, but St. Paul's dome is still the second-largest church dome in the world.

One feature remains from the pre-1666 cathedral. During the fire, a statue of poet John Donne supposedly crashed through the floor and landed in the crypt below. The statue was rescued and placed in the new cathedral. Visitors today can see scorch marks on the base of the statue. St. Paul's has been tested by fire throughout the ages.

An enduring image of the present cathedral is a famous photograph of St. Paul's standing intact while the surrounding section of London burns during a World War II bombing raid. Children can read about the heroic men of the cathedral's fire watch who, instead of hiding in bomb shelters during the Blitz, risked their lives putting out fires in St. Paul's. Without them the cathedral might not have survived.

Wars, fires, and hundreds of years of wear and tear had taken their toll on Christopher Wren's masterpiece. To mark the 300th anniversary of the cathedral in 2010, St. Paul's underwent a £40 million cleaning and repair project, leaving the building in its best shape since the seventeenth century.

Admission to St. Paul's includes a multimedia guide—an upgrade to the usual audio guide found at many historic locations. A family version of the guide lets kids search for hidden secrets, answer quizzes, and play with videos and other interactive content. A cathedral full of tourists staring at video screens may be disconcerting, but for parents

trying to keep children engaged, the multimedia guides are a lifesaver. There is also a mini-cinema in the basement that shows films about St. Paul's on multiple screens.

St. Paul's, like Westminster Abbey, is both a historic site and a functioning church. Although visitors may remember the funeral of Princess Diana held in Westminster Abbey, St. Paul's was the location of Diana's wedding to Charles—a happier moment (or so it seemed at the time). Coronations are the purview of Westminster Abbey, but once enthroned, monarchs often celebrate birthdays and jubilees at St. Paul's.

St. Paul's is an active church and it is closed to visitors at unexpected times. During one visit to the cathedral, we were ushered out because of the arrival of hundreds of Girl Guides (the British version of Girl Scouts) attending a service to mark scouting's anniversary. Although we didn't get to see much of St. Paul's that day, it was a great opportunity for our daughter, who was a girl scout at the time, to make connections with her English comrades.

There is a café and restaurant in the cathedral (no outside food allowed). Most areas are wheelchair accessible and there are toilets and baby changing areas.

Website: www.stpauls.co.uk

Big Wigs

You won't find many wigs in Parliament these days—the Whig party of British politics is long gone, morphed and merged into the current Liberal Party. Wig-wearing legislators were once the norm here, but changing fashions and parliamentary reform have done away with bewigged parliamentarians. Children who have studied government in school may be interested in visiting Britain's Houses of Parliament. If not, parents who want to see Parliament can always remind kids that it is a chance to explore the building where Big Ben is located.

Parliament and Big Ben

Not to shatter any illusions, but Big Ben is not really Big Ben. This symbol of London is actually the clock tower of the Palace of

Westminster. "Big Ben" simply refers to a bell inside the tower. That architectural fact hardly stops people from calling the tower Big Ben, though. The origin of the nickname is not clear, but some historians claim that the clock was named after Sir Benjamin Hall, a supervisor during the construction of the tower. In 2012, to mark the Diamond Jubilee of Queen Elizabeth II, the tower was officially renamed the Elizabeth Tower, but everyone still calls it Big Ben.

The Parliament building interior is amazing and the historical trivia associated with it is fascinating. In the House of Commons chamber, visitors learn the possible origin of the expression "to toe the line." A line is marked on the floor of the chamber, and no matter how vehement the debate, opposing speakers may not step across this line. The line allegedly kept opposing members separated by at least a sword's length. Although swords are gone, disorderly conduct can still be a problem in the chamber, and the House of Commons' sergeant-at-arms has extraordinary powers to maintain the peace. He can issue an arrest warrant for anyone in the country and imprison the unfortunate individual for up to five years without possibility of appeal. You do not want to cross this guy, so toe the line!

In the central dome between the House of Commons and House of Lords, gold murals depict four saints representing the four countries of the United Kingdom: Saint David for Wales, Saint Patrick for Ireland, Saint Andrew for Scotland, and Saint George for England. Another impressive feature of Parliament is the huge, medieval Westminster  Hall. This is the oldest surviving piece of the original Westminster Palace built in 1097. Unlike some restored ancient buildings, Westminster Hall actually looks like a medieval hall, with a high hammer beam ceiling and dark, smoke-stained atmosphere. There are no elaborate furnishings, no bright gold ornamentation, just the cold stonework and a dark wood ceiling. But keep on looking heavenwards—Westminster Hall has one of the world's most impressive collections of medieval roof angels. The carved wooden figures date from around the year 1400.

At the top of the stairs leading from Westminster Hall to St. Stephen's Hall, pause and look up. In 2016, a beautiful new stained glass light sculpture was installed here. It celebrates women's voting rights.

Because of security concerns and the need to keep tourists from bothering members while the legislature is in session, full access to Parliament is limited. British citizens can often get building passes through their MPs (members of Parliament). When Parliament is in session, foreign visitors are limited to what were once called "strangers galleries" in both houses of Parliament. Visitors are no longer referred to as strangers, and the galleries are now known as the "public galleries." How democratic!

Understanding the best way to tour Parliament is no simple task. Public openings are usually held in August and September. Tours are also offered on Saturdays throughout the year. There are occasional Friday evening guided tours of the House of Lords and daytime tours

of the portrait gallery in the House of Commons' modern Portcullis House.

Generally, Parliament is in session Monday through Thursday with lots of holiday breaks. Politicians are the same everywhere and they need plenty of time to schmooze with the electorate back home. The liveliest time to visit is during Question Time, when members verbally parry and the opposition tries to zing the prime minister. Question Time is so popular that only British citizens with tickets stand a chance of getting in, although overseas visitors are admitted if space is available.

Tourists without advance tickets can line up outside St. Stephen's entrance to Parliament, but a wait of one or two hours is common. Sometimes it is easier to get in during the late afternoon or early evening, or on a Friday. When Parliament is in session, there are separate lines for entering the House of Commons and the House of Lords. How can you tell if Parliament is in session? If the tower opposite Big Ben has a flag flying, Parliament is in session. Can these hours change? Of course—they are set by politicians. Check the Parliament website to determine the best time and way to visit.

When all is said and done, the question remains: will kids enjoy a tour of Parliament? The answer is a definite maybe. There are no interactive exhibits here (thumbs down), but no old dead guys either (thumbs up).

There are toilets and baby changing areas and a coffee shop in the Parliament complex. A few parts of the site are not wheelchair accessible. Expect airport-style security screening. Large bags and packages are prohibited and there are no storage facilities onsite.

Website: www.parliament.uk/visiting

Parliamentary Jewels

If you can't get into Parliament, you can at least visit an exhibit on the history of Parliament in the nearby fourteenth-century Jewel Tower, part of the old Palace of Westminster. The Jewel Tower was built around 1365 and it is one of the few surviving buildings from the original Palace. This is a small museum that explains the Jewel Tower's history and it includes a model of the medieval Palace of Westminster.

There is a coffee shop and outdoor picnic tables. No toilets onsite and most of the building is not wheelchair accessible.

Website: www.english-heritage.org.uk

Parliamentary Side Trips — In Search of Abe Lincoln and Ben Franklin

It is a long way from a Kentucky log cabin to London, but a statue of President Abraham Lincoln stands in Parliament Square near Westminster Abbey. This is hardly a major tourist attraction, but it makes an interesting footnote. And seeing Lincoln's statue is one way that American children can make a London connection to US history. In fact, statues of famous Americans are fairly common in London. George Washington's statue is located in front of the National Gallery; Franklin Roosevelt and Winston Churchill share a park bench at the end of Grafton Street; another statue of FDR stands in Grosvenor Square near a statue of Dwight Eisenhower. Roosevelt and Eisenhower were joined in 2011 by a larger-than-life statue of Ronald Reagan. A bust of John F. Kennedy is located near Regent's Park.

Benjamin Franklin House

One famous American hero spent more time in London than Washington, Roosevelt, and Eisenhower combined. Benjamin Franklin lived for almost eighteen years at a house on Craven Street, about a half-mile north of Parliament. While in London, Franklin (a "big Ben" in his own time) invented a twenty-four-hour clock and bifocal glasses. His efforts at diplomacy proved less successful, and Franklin beat a hasty retreat from London in 1775 just ahead of war between Britain and the American colonies.

After Franklin's departure, the house served as an anatomy school (specimens are on display), hotel, and office space. The building fell into disrepair, but the Benjamin Franklin House was restored in 2006 and opened to the public for interpretative tours and as an educational center.

If Benjamin Franklin were reincarnated today he would instantly recognize 36 Craven Street, especially the building's interior, restored to its mid-1700s appearance. The Benjamin Franklin House emphasizes experiences rather than artifacts to transport visitors into Franklin's world. A costumed guide escorts guests through the house while interacting with sound and video snippets portraying Franklin's life in London. The hands-on educational center offers visitors the chance to learn about Franklin's contributions to science. The center is open to groups by appointment. There are toilets onsite. The building is not wheelchair accessible.

Website: www.benjaminfranklinhouse.org

Flowers and Buskers

Covent Garden Market

The Covent Garden Market figures prominently in the musical *My Fair Lady*, whose central character, Eliza Doolittle, was a nineteenth-century flower girl. But Covent Garden's history, like most of London's, is much older. In medieval times, monks from Westminster Abbey grew and sold vegetables in this area, and the name Covent Garden is supposedly a corruption of convent garden—a reference to the abbey.

There were fruit, vegetable, and flower markets at Covent Garden from the medieval era until 1974. When the markets moved out, they were replaced by the modern incarnation of Covent Garden: an entertaining variety of shops, cafés, and restaurants. The area houses an eclectic collection of stores, pubs, theaters, and a museum or two.

On many afternoons and evenings, visitors will find a variety of street performers, or buskers, in the piazza near the old market. The shows are free, but drop some pence into the hat if you appreciate the entertainment. Over several trips, our kids gawked at fire-eaters, a man who danced and spun on his head (wearing a helmet), and a thick-skinned individual who lay down on a bed of nails and invited an audience member to walk on his stomach. Does the admonition "Don't try this at home" sound familiar?

Your family may already know the story of one of Covent Garden's most famous busking duos. The book *A Street Cat Named Bob* tells the tale of a homeless man and his beloved cat. The book was made into a movie in 2016. Covent Garden's reputation for street performances goes back a long time. In 1642, famed British diarist Samuel Pepys wrote about seeing a Punch and Judy marionette show at Covent Garden. If you're in the area in mid-May, be sure to catch the annual Covent Garden May Fayre and Puppet Festival.

The merchants operating in Covent Garden have become a bit less unique in recent years as corporate giants like Apple, Disney, and Gap have muscled aside some independent retailers. Despite this trend, Covent Garden retains enough of its quirkiness to distinguish itself from the average shopping area.

In nice weather, eat outside at one of Covent Garden's cafés. The food varies in type, quality, and cost, but this is generally a good place to find kid-friendly fare. Covent Garden has a number of takeaway shops and full-fledged restaurants.

Covent Garden is more than just an old marketplace, however. The streets around this area, especially northwest toward Seven Dials, are a warren of shops, bars, and restaurants. Stop by Neil's Yard Dairy for a high-cholesterol treat. The dairy shop offers one of the most extensive cheese selections in the city.

For a break from the hustle and bustle, buy some takeaway food from the marketplace and seek out a quiet bench in the churchyard of St. Paul's Church. This unassuming little building is known as the Actors' Church because of its long-standing association with the theater community in Covent Garden and the nearby West End theater district.

After dark, especially on weekends, the crowds around Covent Garden are full of barhoppers. Some spill out onto the streets and it can be a little disconcerting when walking through the area with young children, but the revelers are generally unthreatening. On some summer weekends, the streets are so overrun with tourists and partiers that Transport for London restricts access to the Covent Garden Tube station. Not to worry—it is an easy walk to Leicester Square, or even to Trafalgar Square, where you can catch the Tube or a bus.

Transport Museum

Right next to Covent Garden's central market is a museum that attracts children like a magnet. Where else in London can kids get behind the controls of a subway train and take a virtual journey through the tunnels of London's Underground? At the Transport Museum, kids and adults can climb on old trams and buses, "drive" several vintages of Tube trains, and buy popular London Transport souvenirs. The museum employs costumed actors who interact with—and occasionally startle—young visitors.

The Transport Museum has areas where younger children can push buttons, spin signs, and generally touch and play with everything. This is the most popular family-friendly attraction in Covent Garden. There are interactive galleries, simulators, and displays of many buses, trams, and other conveyances from the Transport Museum's huge collection.

All Aboard! is designed to let children under age six climb onto

scaled-down versions of a bus, Tube train, and taxi. The Interchange is a hands-on exploration area for seven- to eleven-year-olds. The museum also features an activity room where kids can grab some crayons and color transportation-related pictures. The museum's shop is the place to purchase Transport for London merchandise. If your kids love buses, streetcars, and subways, the Transport Museum is worth a visit.

There are cafés and an indoor picnic room onsite along with toilets and baby changing areas. The museum, and most of the collection, is wheelchair accessible.

Website: www.ltmuseum.co.uk

The Royal Opera House

The Royal Opera House is located just behind Covent Garden Market. Most performances here are intended for adults, but occasionally the Royal Opera offers programs for children. Check the opera's website at www.roh.org.uk

War and Peace

Churchill War Rooms

The story of Winston Churchill seems to be onscreen everywhere: *Churchill* (2017), *The Darkest Hour* (2017), *Dunkirk* (2017). One of the best places to get behind the scenes of the Churchill story is at London's Churchill War Rooms. This was the underground headquarters of Winston Churchill during the World War II Blitz attacks on the city.

Most kids like exploring hidden areas, so the whole family will probably appreciate meandering through the warren of underground conference rooms, passageways, sleeping quarters, communications centers, and map rooms. For a little education along with your exploration, use the audio headphones provided free with each admission. There is a special audio tour for kids, and the War Rooms' website has a downloadable trail map for children. The commentary isn't boring, and listening to it slows down kids who tend to fast-forward through historical displays.

The Churchill War Rooms are historically authentic. After the war ended, many of the rooms were closed off and left untouched for years. The Imperial War Museum, which operates the Churchill War Rooms, has done a thorough job of restoring the site to its wartime appearance.

Almost the entire wartime underground complex is open to the public. The Churchill family's private quarters include Mrs. Churchill's bedroom, a private dining room, and a kitchen. The museum transports visitors through Churchill's life, although it's not a strictly chronological review. Instead, the museum presents five thematic chapters: Young Churchill, War Leader, Cold War Statesman, Maverick Politician, and Wilderness Years.

There's more British historical detail here than the average non-British visitor may wish to absorb, and the Churchill Museum may be a bit dry for some children. But the museum makes use of computer and video technology to enliven that history for the casual visitor while allowing history buffs to delve deeper into the story. The spine of the museum is Lifeline, a fifty-foot-long video table that presents an interactive timeline of Churchill's life. Visitors can explore more than 300 data points, encountering some programmed "Easter egg" surprises that will delight, or at least startle, those gathered around the huge video screen.

The museum interactively captures a few of Churchill's personality quirks. The man was fond of the carp stocked in the fishpond at his family home. He would dangle his hand on the water's surface, where

the fish would gently nibble his fingers. The museum has a tiny "pond," and electronic fish appear when a visitor touches the Plexiglas surface. Churchill ranks as one of the most quotable speakers of the twentieth century, and the museum resounds with recordings of his speeches. Exhibits also include a captured Enigma machine that helped break German wartime codes. The story of the code-breaking effort was brought to the screen in *The Imitation Game* (2014). Churchill referred to the code breaking team as "the geese that laid the golden eggs and never cackled."

Other artifacts on display include Churchill's odd-looking siren suit: custom-made velvet engineer's coveralls that he preferred as casual wear. Uniforms, document reproductions, and a model of Churchill's Chartwell home are also on display. Near the end of the museum stands a front door from No. 10 Downing Street, a poignant reminder of the man who twice served as prime minister.

The museum has a café (no outside food allowed) and there are toilets and baby changing areas. The museum is wheelchair accessible.

Website: www.iwm.org.uk (search under "Churchill War Rooms")

Imperial War Museum London

London has an entire museum devoted to war—the Imperial War Museum. This museum tries not to glamorize war; in fact, there are a few fairly graphic displays, such as the Holocaust Exhibition, that are not suitable for younger children. What the Imperial War Museum does offer is a wealth of historic hardware: guns, tanks, airplanes, and rockets.

To commemorate the centenary of World War I (1914–1918), the Imperial War Museum underwent a major transformation with the opening of the First World War Galleries. A Life at the Front exhibit provides a realistic depiction of the sights and sounds of life and death in World War I trenches. This area displays an iconic Sopwith Camel biplane and a once-lumbering Mark V tank. The museum's soaring atrium features dramatic large displays including a Harrier jet, a Spitfire fighter plane, a Russian tank, and a V-2 rocket.

World War II had a devastating impact on many London residents. What was it like to live through war in London? A Family in Wartime traces the experiences of an ordinary family who endured wartime rationing, evacuation of their children, and bombings of their south London home. The exhibit makes history personal—lessons that won't be lost on modern families.

The Imperial War Museum gives visitors a British perspective of World War II. Britain's defeat at Dunkirk, the Blitz, and the Battle of Britain become much more real after a visit to the Imperial War Museum.

The museum has a café with children's menus, outside picnic area, toilets and baby changing areas, and coat/package check. Most areas of the museum are wheelchair accessible. Admission is free.

Website: www.iwm.org.uk (search under "IWM London")

Florence Nightingale Museum

Lo! in that house of misery,

A lady with a lamp I see,

Pass through the glimmering gloom,

And flit from room to room.

—"Santa Filomena" by Henry Wadsworth Longfellow

The Florence Nightingale Museum portrays another side of warfare—that of mercy and dedication in the face of misery. Florence Nightingale was the "lady with a lamp," a heroic British nurse during and after the Crimean War. The museum's collection displays artifacts from that conflict, Nightingale's childhood, and her later life as a health reform campaigner. The museum includes modern interactive displays. Kids can don stethoscopes and listen at audio hot spots scattered throughout the exhibits.

This little museum is popular with school groups and it can occasionally be crowded. At other times, this is a low-key and worthwhile stop for children or adults who are interested in nursing and in the Florence Nightingale story.

There are toilets onsite and the museum is wheelchair accessible.

Website: www.florence-nightingale.co.uk

Museums—
Some Serious Some Not

He gazed and gazed and gazed and gazed,

Amazed, amazed, amazed, amazed.

—"Rhyme for a Child Viewing a Naked Venus in a Painting" by Robert Browning

Realistically, many kids have little patience to devote to art exhibits and museums. When you plan your visit to London, consider limiting the time you spend in museums and the number of things you try to see. Be prepared to miss a lot; kids often fast-forward through museums, leaving placard-reading parents in their wake. Satisfy yourself with seeing the highlights and getting the flavor of each museum. With luck, you will return to London and see more when the kids are older.

London has dozens of museums, some more interesting to families than others. We'll get you started with this handful:

- The world-renowned British Museum, located in north-central London
- A cluster of three very different museums—Natural History, Science, and Victoria and Albert—in South Kensington
- The Museum of London, near London's financial district
- The Museum of London Docklands
- The Victoria and Albert Museum of Childhood—a museum devoted to toys
- A museum dedicated to the world-famous fictional detective Sherlock Holmes

- The Tate Modern, the National Gallery, and the Courtauld Gallery, for families who want to venture into art museums
- The Postal Museum—where you ride on the previously "secret" underground postal railroad
- The Charles Dickens Museum—it is the best of museums, it is the worst of museums

British Museum

When I first came up to London I had rooms in Montague Street, just around the corner from the British Museum, and there I waited, filling in my too abundant leisure time by studying all those branches of science which might make me more efficient.

—*The Memoirs of Sherlock Holmes* by Sir Arthur Conan Doyle

The British Museum is the most famous museum in England—perhaps in the world—and it has a lot to offer from a child's perspective. But

the British Museum is so large that it can overwhelm visiting families and quickly go from a thrilling experience to a tiring one. Here are some survival strategies. Focus on a few museum highlights, pick a theme and look for things that appeal to your child's special interests. Or you can sign up for a ninety-minute guided highlights tour.

Read up on the British Museum before you go. Nothing is quite as pathetic as tourists with young children standing in the lobby, studying a map, trying to decide which way to head in this vast museum. The kids start getting antsy, the parents become frazzled, and the visit is off to a bad start. A high-tech solution is to rent children's multimedia guides, or take advantage of low-tech options and pick up free family trail guides or activity backpacks from the families desk in the Great Court.

The British Museum was founded in 1753, making even the museum a "museum piece." Despite its age, the British Museum continues to evolve. It has long-standing permanent displays from Egypt, western Asia, Greece, and Rome; prehistoric and Roman-era British artifacts; and extensive medieval, Renaissance, and modern collections.

The museum is chock-full of iconic exhibits, but the largest crowds inevitably gather around the Rosetta Stone. Undeniably important as an artifact, the stone can disappoint children who manage to wiggle through the masses for an up close view.

Although most museums have strict hands-off policies concerning their exhibits, the British Museum features Hands On desks. Located in the central Reading Room and other areas of the museum, Hands On offers a chance to touch and examine a select (and presumably sturdy) sample of ancient artifacts. The museum's Digital Discovery Centre is an attempt to bridge the gap between traditional museum content and the digital age. The center offers weekend activities geared to families with children age five and older.

The museum has a restaurant and cafés (no outside food allowed), and a family picnic area is open on weekends. Coat checks, baby changing areas and a nursing area are available. Most of the British Museum is wheelchair accessible. Admission is free, except for some special exhibits.

Website: www.britishmuseum.org

Natural History Museum

There are natural history museums in many major cities, and London is no exception. Although there is nothing uniquely British about this museum, the London version is superb. Volcanoes, dinosaurs, and ecology—natural history is a natural magnet for children. But like many museums, the Natural History Museum must compete for the attention of children and adults who are used to seeing elaborate computer graphics and animation. The Natural

History Museum still succeeds in getting a "wow" out of visitors who have already seen dinosaurs come to life through movie magic.

Exhibits include some realistic animated dinosaurs, a simulated womb, and a Creepy Crawlies exhibit for anthropoid lovers. A huge skeleton of a blue whale is suspended overhead in the museum's central hall, and in another room visitors can experience a simulated earthquake. Some mild cautions: the dinosaurs are munching on a less fortunate fellow; the human biology exhibit may evoke some interesting questions from younger children; if spiders make you uncomfortable, Creepy Crawlies is not for you. The whale is tame, though, and the earthquake is eye opening.

The museum's Darwin Centre houses 22 million specimens, sometimes referred to as "gross stuff in jars." These were collected on the voyages of Captain James Cook, Charles Darwin, and countless other scientists. Kids can get a close-up look at this pickled menagerie on a behind-the-scenes tour. The Darwin Centre's display of insects is housed in a modernistic pod-like building filled with interactive exhibits that practically bring the collection of dead bugs to life.

Not all the specimens at the Natural History Museum are dead, though. The wildlife garden features butterflies, animals, plants, and birds—all very much alive and on display near the museum's west entrance from April through October. Wintertime visitors can rent skates and glide around the museum's outdoor ice-skating rink, open late October through early January. The rink is one of several that operate seasonally near major London attractions.

The Natural History Museum has a hands-on science lab designed for kids ages seven to fourteen. The Investigate Lab lets children use computers, microscopes, and other scientific tools to explore animal, plant, and geological specimens. Parents can also purchase Discovery Guides in versions for kids ages five to seven and eight to eleven. Like the British Museum, the Natural History Museum hosts special events for children and families, including tours, workshops, and even puppet shows. Check the museum's website for the latest offerings.

The museum has a restaurant, cafés, and a snack bar, plus indoor and outdoor picnic areas. There are toilets, baby changing areas, and a coat/bag check. Most of the museum is wheelchair accessible. Admission is free, except for some special exhibits. On weekends and school holidays, there can be long lines to get into the Natural History Museum.

Website: www.nhm.ac.uk

If natural history is a favorite, your family could also add a visit to the diminutive **Horniman Museum and Gardens** located about eight miles south of central London. For information see the museum's website at www.horniman.ac.uk

Victoria and Albert Museum

The Fossil sisters lived in the Cromwell Road. At that end
of it which is farthest away from the Brompton Road, and
yet sufficiently near it so one could be taken to look at the
dolls' houses in the Victoria and Albert every wet day."

—*Ballet Shoes* by Noel Streatfeild

From a child's perspective, the Victoria and Albert Museum is a stark contrast to its neighbors, the Science and Natural History Museums. Go ahead, ask your children if they want to tour a museum featuring exhibits on the history of architecture, fashion, textiles, ceramics, and jewelry. The answer may be no, especially when that museum is so close to all the cool stuff in the Science and Natural History Museums.

Yet the Victoria and Albert Museum staff deserves credit because they try hard to interest children. Young visitors can borrow activity backpacks at the front desk. The backpacks relate to different areas of the museum. Children can discover objects by feel while blindfolded

or go on a treasure hunt. Nothing can turn the V&A into a children's museum, but the backpacks make a family visit manageable. Hands-on exhibits are scattered throughout the museum and an activity cart for children is available on Sundays and some school holidays. In nice weather, children can splash in the V&A's shallow courtyard reflecting pool (assuming it's okay with their parents).

For budding fashion designers or architects, the Victoria and Albert is a must-see. Among the most amazing areas are the Cast Courts— two huge halls filled with life-sized plaster casts of famous statues, cathedral gates, and ancient columns. The size and extent of the collection is impressive and it's hard to keep in mind these are just plaster copies of ancient originals.

The V&A has a café, a restaurant and indoor and outdoor picnic spots. The museum has toilets and baby changing areas/nursing room. A coat and package check is available. Most areas of the museum are wheelchair accessible. Admission is free except for special exhibits.

Website: www.vam.ac.uk

Science Museum

London's Science Museum has such potential—a world-class presentation of science and technology, with interactive exhibits, and just a smidgen of history. Unfortunately, parts of the museum are worn, and "out of order" signs appear frequently. Some of the most interesting activities also have extra admission fees and long lines. Despite these drawbacks, the Science Museum can grab a child's attention like almost no other museum in the city.

Wonderlab is an interactive gallery with zones devoted to mathematics, chemistry, light, electricity, forces, and space. There are dozens of stations, so Wonderlab can accommodate a large crowd of kids, and they can all put their hands on something. Wonderlab is appropriate for older children, but the museum has not forgotten younger kids. The basement Garden is an area where three- to six-year-olds can experiment through play. Pattern Pod is another favorite gallery for kids ages five to eight. There is an admission charge for the flight and space simulator rides that add a bit of amusement park excitement to the Science Museum.

The Science Museum is a popular destination for school groups, and it can get a little crowded at times. If you are visiting while British schools are in session, plan to arrive early or late in the day.

The museum offers indoor areas where groups can eat brown bag lunches. The museum's cafés are acceptable places to grab a snack or light lunch; there are plenty of menu choices for children.

There are toilets, baby changing areas and a coat/bag check. The museum is wheelchair accessible. Admission is free, but donations are encouraged. Special exhibits, the IMAX cinema, flight simulators, and the like all require paid tickets.

Website: www.sciencemuseum.org.uk

Museum of London

London is chock-full of museums dedicated to various forms of art and history. The Museum of London takes an introspective view—the subject is London itself. The museum examines the city from prehistory to present day. This provides a history lesson, showing glimpses of old London from Roman artifacts to re-created eighteenth-century prison cells. And what kid won't peer with morbid fascination at the diorama and video depicting the Great Fire of London?

One of the museum's prize displays is the Lord Mayor's coach. The coach is elaborate, but if you have already visited the Royal Mews at Buckingham Palace, you may have seen enough ceremonial coaches for one trip.

The Museum of London is a good rainy-day venue for older children and adults. The Sackler Hall on the lower level has computers where visitors can learn more about the museum's massive inventory of London-related objects. Frequent special exhibits can attract crowds and may require advanced tickets.

The Museum of London is built along the old Roman city wall, a portion of which forms one side of the inner courtyard. Thousands of fascinating artifacts from the abandoned Roman city of Londinium are on display.

There is a restaurant and an indoor picnic area. Coat check, toilets and baby changing areas are available. The museum is wheelchair accessible. In 2022, the Museum of London moves to a new location at historic Smithfield Market.

Website: www.museumoflondon.org.uk

Museum of London Docklands

A great deal of London's history revolves around its position at the center of Britain's seagoing empire. The Museum of London Docklands is housed in a restored 200-year-old Georgian warehouse at Canary Wharf. The museum contains countless artifacts that tell the story of London's ship docks, warehouses, and seagoing trade. It is not always a pretty picture, as you will learn in the exhibition on slave trade: London, Sugar & Slavery.

The museum's Sailortown gallery is a full-scale re-creation of the dark and dubious local streetscape frequented by sailors in the mid-1800s. But the Mudlarks gallery may be more appropriate for younger children. Mudlarks are people who search the muddy banks of the Thames looking for treasure, usually finding junk, but occasionally unearthing valuable artifacts. The Mudlarks gallery contains an

interactive play area for children up to age eight. Despite the "dirty" name, no actual mud digging is involved. Be sure to pick up free timed entry Mudlarks gallery tickets as you enter the museum.

There is a café, restaurant and indoor picnic area. Lockers, toilets and baby changing areas are available. The museum is wheelchair accessible. Admission is free.

Website: www.museumoflondon.org.uk
           (select "Museum of London Docklands")

Victoria and Albert Museum of Childhood

This branch of the Victoria and Albert Museum claims to house one of the largest toy collections in the world. It certainly has an impressive array of dolls, dollhouses, stuffed animals, games, trains, puppets, and costumes. Although many exhibits are static do-not-touch displays of toy antiquity, the Museum of Childhood offers areas where visiting children can actually play with toys. Children under age five will enjoy the indoor sandbox and locations where they can dress in costumes,

set up and knock down blocks, and play with dollhouses. There are drop-in activities and a board game area. Because of its location in east London, the Museum of Childhood is out of the way for many tourists, but it is a popular venue for local school groups.

Admission to the museum is free. There is a café (no outside food allowed), picnic area, toilets and baby changing areas, coat and package check. The museum is wheelchair accessible.

Website: www.museumofchildhood.org.uk

Sherlock Holmes Museum

Are you sure that Sherlock Holmes was a fictional character? Using your powers of inductive reasoning, you may have determined that Mr. Holmes is indeed a fake. This museum is a fake, too; an elaborate, fun, and almost believable fake filled with Sherlock Holmes memorabilia. In the famous detective's study, kids can put on a deerstalker hat, pick up a meerschaum pipe, and utter the inevitable "Elementary, my dear Watson" to their hearts' content.

The Sherlock Holmes Museum has a gift shop and toilets onsite, but no other facilities. Most areas of the museum are not wheelchair accessible. For information see the museum's website at www.sherlock-holmes.co.uk

Rejuvenated interest in the world's most famous fictional detective—literature, movies, and television series—is good news for anyone looking for a Sherlock experience in London. If you emerge from the museum seeking more landmarks for this enduring character, check out some other London locations:

- Look for the Sherlock Holmes motif on the walls of Baker Street Underground station. The nine-foot-high bronze statue of the detective standing outside the station is also hard to miss.
- Speedy's Café, the sandwich shop frequented by Holmes and Watson in the BBC's *Sherlock* series, is a real café on Gower Street, near Euston rail station. In the series, the Gower Street location is the stand-in for 221b Baker Street. The café serves Sherlock-themed snacks.
- The Sherlock Holmes Pub is a short walk from Charing Cross Underground and rail stations. This is where Holmes tracked down Francis Hay Moulton in *The Noble Bachelors*. Inside the pub there's a replica of Holmes' study, Sherlock memorabilia, and Dr. Watson's old service revolver.
- Other literary locations and favorite Holmes haunts include the British Museum, Royal Opera House, and the Lyceum Theatre.

Special Delivery

A secret railway snakes under central London. No, it's not some unknown branch of the London Underground, this is a small-scale railway. The London Postal Rail network—Mail Rail—is seventy feet below the surface, in tunnels just seven-feet wide, and it hits breakneck speeds of almost eight miles per hour. Once a vital link for delivering mail in central London, the Mail Rail system was abandoned in 2003, but a short section has been restored as the star attraction of London's Postal Museum. The museum also showcases the history of Britain's postal service. Everyone loves riding the train, but younger children will also have fun in the mini-town postal play area.

The museum is about a mile south of King's Cross rail station and a short stroll east of Coram's Fields. There are lockers, toilets, baby changing facilities and a café onsite. Except for the Mail Rail ride, the museum is wheelchair accessible.

Website: www.postalmuseum.org

Charles Dickens Museum

Oliver Twist, *Pickwick Papers* and *Nicholas Nickleby*...all classics of English literature and stories that many children encounter in school. The Charles Dickens Museum brings to life the house where the author wrote those three famous works. Visiting families can pick up a family trail guide designed for kids between four- and twelve-years-old. Children will also enjoy the hands-on equipment in the basement Victorian kitchen. The museum has costumes for dress-up and a toy theater where kids can put on a play.

There are toilets and a café onsite, but no bag storage. Four of five floors in the museum are wheelchair accessible.

Website: www.dickensmuseum.com

When planning a day out, note that the Dickens Museum, Coram's Fields, and the Postal Museum are all within a five-minute walk of each other.

An Art Museum—
or Two or Three

For many kids, visiting art museums can be challenging. Some budding young artists are fascinated by art museums, but you know your children best. For families who want to include an art stop, London offers a wealth of choices. The Tate Modern and the National Gallery are among the finest big-scale art museums in London. The Courtauld Gallery is a little gem that just might suit families looking for art in a smaller dose.

Tate Modern

It's worth a visit to the Tate Modern just to see the building. This former power plant sits on the bank of the Thames at the south end of the Millennium Bridge near the Globe Theatre. The scale of the building is awe-inspiring. Visitors feel dwarfed in the huge turbine hall that once housed massive electrical generating equipment. The displays are often impressive simply because of their scale.

The Tate offers a dedicated welcome room for families, and there is a studio where kids can take part in artistic activities. Many children will also enjoy the interactive digital drawing area. There are special

programs for older children (check the Tate's website for schedules). Families can rent a multimedia guide to use while touring the museum. The Tate's website also has downloadable apps that turn museum visits into hunt-and-seek adventures.

The Tate has one of the best observation decks in London. It's not as high as the View from the Shard, but the 360-degree outdoor balcony at the top of the Tate's new Blavatnik Building is a great place to see the London skyline. Best of all, like the rest of the Tate Modern, it's free.

The Tate Modern's café and restaurant offer welcome respite after touring the galleries (there is a children's menu.) The museum has toilets on every floor, all with baby changing areas. There is also a baby care/nursing room. The Tate Modern is wheelchair accessible.

Website: www.tate.org.uk (select "Tate Modern")

National Gallery

Overlooking busy Trafalgar Square, Britain's National Gallery has a permanent collection that spans the art universe from the mid-

1400s to 1900. There are iconic paintings here, such as one of Van Gogh's Sunflowers, and a number of works by Britain's own J. M. W. Turner. The National Gallery's collection is vast, with more than 2,300 masterpieces on public display. Visiting families may want to take a museum highlights tour, such as "Impressionism and Beyond," featuring several key artists. The gallery also offers family audio tours, printed trail guides, and downloadable apps.

The National Gallery's education center, located on Orange Street at the rear of the building, has baby changing areas, toilets, and a street-level entryway into the site. On weekends and during holidays, families can check coats and other items here. Most family-oriented special events are held in the education center.

The museum has a café and restaurant. Picnic lunches are allowed in the education center and in the foyer outside the Gallery's Sainsbury Wing. There are toilets on most levels and the museum has two coat/bag check rooms. Most of the museum is wheelchair accessible.

Website: www.nationalgallery.org.uk

Courtauld Gallery

If other art museums overwhelm your family by their sheer size and vastness of their collections, here's an alternative. The Courtauld Gallery presents stellar art on a human scale. The Courtauld collection includes just over 500 paintings; London's National Gallery has more than 2,000.

Famous paintings by Monet, Gauguin and Van Gogh, along with Renaissance masterpieces, are arranged throughout the Courtauld's four moderately sized levels. Even for museum-averse children, a tour of the Courtauld is hardly an endurance test. For art lovers of all ages, the gallery is a must-see gem.

The gallery has a café, storage lockers, and toilets. The Courtauld is wheelchair accessible.

Website: www.courtauld.ac.uk

Fun But Tacky

London is full of historic sites, top-notch museums, and cultural icons. But not every venue falls squarely into one of these categories. The city has its share of tacky and kitschy attractions.

Madame Tussaud's Wax Museum—*Gee, Don't They Look Lifelike*?

Not everyone is a fan of wax museums. There is something weird and macabre about these worlds of wax. After all, Madame Tussaud began her career by displaying the death masks of people executed during the French Revolution. Fortunately, today's visitors to Madame Tussaud's are treated to less horror and more entertainment—musicians, sports figures, and other famous folk.

Wax figures are lifelike, but they lack certain human qualities, such as mortality and ego, so the museum can create some combinations that would be improbable in real life. There is nothing to prevent Kim Kardashian from communing with Vincent Van Gogh or Albert Einstein from kibitzing with Donald Trump. To our knowledge, the museum has yet to display those unlikely combinations, but at one time Madame Tussaud's enabled King Henry VIII to gather all his wives together in one room without anyone losing her head. Children visiting from abroad will recognize many of the figures in the museum, but perhaps not every British sports star or politician.

Museum visitors can climb into the shell of a London taxi and take a brief ride highlighting the city's history. In a couple of minutes, you are whisked past the Great Fire, the building of St. Paul's, the Victorian era, the Blitz, and back to present-day London. Good news—no taxi driver, so no tip is required.

Madame Tussaud's is one of the most visited attractions in London.

Lines to get in are often long, but they move fairly fast. Because it is more than 200 years old, Madame Tussaud's almost qualifies as a historic site itself, albeit a very commercial one.

There are several food and drink stands onsite. Toilets and a stroller/buggy storage room are available. Many areas are accessible, but wheelchair users should book tickets in advance.

Website: www.madametussauds.com/london

London Dungeon—Tackiness and Terror

The London Dungeon has always been scary, gory, fun, and macabre... pick your adjective. The dungeon moved in 2013, allowing the operators to boast about a newer, bigger, bolder, and better attraction. While "bolder and better" is subjective, the dungeon is certainly newer and bigger at its current site near the London Eye.

Parents traveling with young children should be aware that venues like this are designed to frighten the daylights out of most kids and many adults. London has at least three offenders: the Clink Prison Museum, the innocently named London Bridge Experience, and the London Dungeon.

To give you an idea of just how perverse the London Dungeon is, here's a description taken from an old visitor's guide:

Exhibition depicting the darker side of British Medieval History, Death, Torture, Damnation and Disease. The dark, slimy vaults contain Trials by Ordeal, History of Capital Punishment and the Tortures used in the Tower of London...A major attraction is The Jack the Ripper Experience—a 20 minute multi-media exhibition...Also on display are the "headcrushers" from France and the Spanish "garrotters."

Need we say more? To see real dungeons, without all the plastic gore, bad acting and histrionics, head for the Tower of London.

There are toilets onsite (and that's a good thing). Most areas of the London Dungeon are wheelchair accessible. Some rides have health and physical restrictions.

Website: www.thedungeons.com/london

Shrek's Adventure

You can run away from the London Dungeon's screaming hordes and pay a visit to an ogre at County Hall. Although prone to frightening roars and known for grumpiness, this particular ogre is Shrek, a character beloved by children worldwide. DreamWorks has applied its animation magic to recreate the kingdom of Far, Far Away with live shows, rides and appearances by Shrek and friends. Shrek's Adventure London is targeted at children ages six through twelve (and their parents). Some of the site is wheelchair accessible, although there are restrictions.

Website: www.shreksadventure.com/london

On the River

Britain's maritime history is well represented along the banks of the River Thames by two ships in particular—one that circumnavigated the globe in the sixteenth century and one that fought sea battles in the twentieth century.

Golden Hinde

The Golden Hinde is a nautical tourist attraction along the south bank of the Thames. The Hinde is a full-scale reconstruction of the sixteenth-century ship that Sir Francis Drake sailed around the world. The ship is moored at St. Mary Overie Dock, just up the river from London Bridge. Like the original, the new Golden Hinde sailed around the world, but the modern ship started its journey in California in 1973.

Sailing history buffs will appreciate the Golden Hinde because Sir Francis Drake's accomplishments personify the height of British sea power. Children may wish to stop here just to climb around the ship. Those who want to get more in touch with the salty life of tall ship sailing can arrange to spend the night onboard during one of the Golden Hinde's occasional living history events. Berths are on the hard wooden lower decks, so bring a pillow!

Website: www.goldenhinde.co.uk

HMS Belfast

While standing on Tower Bridge, you can't miss the huge warship anchored just upstream in the Thames. The HMS Belfast is a retired World War II cruiser, now open to the public and operated as a floating museum by the Imperial War Museum. The ship saw action in the D-Day invasion and later during the Korean War.

If you are a warship aficionado and you are in the neighborhood, stop by the Belfast. Few kids can resist the chance to explore the maze of decks, passageways, and compartments in this old ship. There are free audio guides, including a family-focused guide. Check the HMS

Belfast website for occasional special events and exhibits.

Children under age sixteen get in free. There is a café onboard and a restaurant on the ship's pier. Toilets are available, but no coat check. Strollers/pushchairs are restricted to certain areas of the ship. Parts of the Belfast are not wheelchair accessible.

Website: www.iwm.org.uk (search on "HMS Belfast")

Southwark Cathedral

Although it is little known to tourists, Southwark Cathedral is one of the finest medieval churches in London. Approaching the church, it is hard to ignore the stark contrast between this ancient London cathedral and the ultra-modern Shard tower looming barely 1,000 feet away. But step inside and leave modern London behind. Southwark Cathedral is the oldest cathedral building in London and there has been a church on the site since at least the year 606.

Local resident John Harvard was baptized in the cathedral in 1607—he went on to found Harvard University. Look for the memorial

to William Shakespeare, who reclines below a stained glass window depicting characters from many of his plays.

In the churchyard there is a monument to Native American chief

Mahomet Weyonomon. This Mohegan leader traveled to London in 1735 to petition the king for the return of tribal lands seized by English settlers in the Connecticut colony. Weyonomon died of smallpox during his visit and he was buried in an unmarked grave near the cathedral. Queen Elizabeth II dedicated this unusual monument in 2006.

Website: www.cathedral.southwark.anglican.org

London Experiences

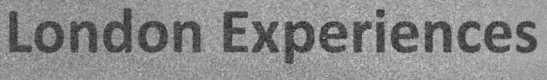

71

Go to the Park

I want always to be a little boy and to have
fun. So I ran away to Kensington Gardens and
lived a long long time among the fairies.

—*Peter Pan* by J. M. Barrie

London has some of the most beautiful parks and some of the most awesome playgrounds in the world. Stroll through them as a family and everyone is happy. Adults can admire English gardening miracles while children run and play. Never underestimate the value of simply sitting on a park bench and soaking up the atmosphere of London. Unless it is raining—that's not the "atmosphere" you'll want to soak up. In warm weather, lawn chairs are spread across London's expansive parks. A word of caution: if you sit down in a lawn chair, you have rented that chair. To relax for free, sit on a park bench or a picnic cloth.

While parents may carefully plan an overseas trip, sometimes kids would rather stay home. Because you are reading this book, you may have already chosen to ignore this truth. You are sure that a visit to London will be an educational, horizon-broadening experience for the whole family. You are absolutely correct, but don't forget to have fun. Let your kids explore London's playgrounds and parks as part of the trip.

For visitors with young children, playgrounds serve two purposes. First, they are a good break from an intense schedule of sightseeing. Forced to behave themselves in hotels, restaurants, cathedrals, theaters, and museums, most kids can stand to burn off some energy on a playground. The second purpose of playgrounds is simple bribery. You might be able to get through that last museum gallery if you promise your kids a playground break. Fortunately, visitors do not have to look far for a playground in London because they're located in big parks and shoehorned into tiny lots between buildings.

St. James's Park and Green Park

St. James's Park tops our list as the most beautiful park in central London. Situated between Buckingham Palace and the government offices at Whitehall, St. James's is an island of green surrounded by many of London's prime historic sites. In 1827, John Nash designed the park that visitors see today, but this space has been a royal park since King Henry VIII acquired St. James's in the early sixteenth century.

Modern day St. James's Park has starred, or at least claimed a supporting role, in popular television and movie productions. *Downton Abbey* filmed here twice, and everyone's favorite nanny visits the park in *Mary Poppins Returns* (2018). St. James's Park also made a big movie splash in *101 Dalmatians* (1996) when Dalmatians Pongo and Perdita sent their human masters tumbling into the park's lake. In this same lake, kids can spot pelicans, flamingos, and swans—some of the twenty species of waterfowl that live in the park. Look for the shy, rare black swans at the island nearest Whitehall, hiding beneath overhanging tree branches. All the birds gather around when the park staff feeds the pelicans in the early afternoon.

St. James's Park has just one small playground for younger children to enjoy. But it's the only playground with a direct view of Buckingham Palace, which makes it kind of special.

Green Park is just across the street from St. James's Park, and until recently it was known as Upper St. James's Park. Green Park dates to the 1500s, so "recently" refers to the mid-1700s. Once used as a dueling ground, Green Park is now another pleasant spot with tall trees and broad lawns serving as a serene buffer between the palace and Mayfair's busy Piccadilly thoroughfare.

The flowery grounds of St. James's Park are beautiful to look at, but Green Park is a prime spot to rent a lawn chair and relax. The parks are not all nature and quiet gardens, though. St. James's hosts band concerts in the summer. And the peace and quiet is truly shattered when artillery gun salutes are fired from one of the parks to celebrate a royal birthday or other occasion.

Toilets in Green Park are at the northeast corner near the Green Park Underground station. In St. James's Park, toilets are at the east end near Horse Guards Parade and in the center of the park at Marlborough Gate. There are cafés, a restaurant, and plenty of picnic opportunities. Most areas are wheelchair accessible.

Website: www.royalparks.org.uk

Hyde Park and Kensington Gardens

Hyde Park, along with adjoining Kensington Gardens, is a massive expanse of green in the core of London. Hyde Park dates to the early

1500s, when it was a royal hunting ground. The park packs a wealth of activities kids will enjoy:

- Boating and fishing on the Serpentine lake
- Seasonal swimming from the Lido
- Tennis, lawn bowling, and putting greens
- Biking and horseback riding
- Playgrounds
- Concerts

Boating on Hyde Park's Serpentine is a favorite good-weather activity. A solar-powered shuttle boat silently whisks passengers across the Serpentine. The unique craft operates (weather permitting) on weekends in spring and autumn and daily in summer. Visitors can also rent rowboats and pedal boats from Hyde Park's boathouse.

We've noted that St. James's Park was a playground for Dalmatians Pongo and Perdita. Nearby Kensington Gardens has its own story for children: Peter Pan lived here. He's still here, in fact, and kids will enjoy discovering the Peter Pan sculpture in Kensington Gardens. Don't get too excited, it is just a statue, but if you believe . . .

The search for Peter Pan and his pirates draws long lines of London children to Kensington Gardens, where a popular playground evokes the memory of two of Kensington's most famous residents: Princess Diana and Peter Pan. The Diana Princess of Wales Memorial Playground is on the site of an earlier playground donated by Peter Pan author J. M. Barrie. Kensington Palace was Diana's official home, and the princess often sought anonymous refuge in Kensington Gardens.

But it's the playground, not the memorial or literary connections, that attracts kids. A fully rigged pirate ship seemingly grounded on a beach dominates the two-acre site. Children can climb a hidden passage between the galleon's three decks and even try to refloat the ship by moving sand out of the ballast. The park's beach cove is a water play area where kids can search for the imprints of fossils and even a mermaid's tail...but do watch out for the crocodiles! When children tire of the pirate ship and cove, they can move on to the tree house camp and call each other using the park's "tree phones." Then it's on to the Native American teepees, or maybe a stop in the Movement and Musical Garden to make music, or at least joyful noise. The Peter Pan theme continues in the park's restroom facilities, located in the Home Under the Ground. Can't quite recall Peter Pan's story? Home Under the Ground is where the Lost Boys lived.

Kensington Gardens is essentially a western extension of Hyde Park. Together, the two parks form a green oasis stretching from the backyard of Buckingham Palace all the way to Kensington Palace. Other highlights here are the gardens around Kensington Palace, a model boat pond, a seasonal restaurant, areas for kite flying, and a puppet theater.

The Diana Memorial Fountain is located just south of the Serpentine Bridge in Hyde Park and is one of the most visited areas of any park in London. The Diana Memorial is low-key, as royal monuments go. Contrast it with the nearby ornate Albert Memorial, erected by Queen Victoria to honor her beloved husband Prince Albert.

Your family may also enjoy a brief visit to the two little art galleries located near either end of the Serpentine Bridge. These present art in

small doses, which is a good fit for some children. The galleries have a restaurant, toilets and baby changing rooms. For information, see the gallery's website at www.serpentinegalleries.org

Young equestrians and their parents can gain a different perspective on Hyde Park by signing up for a ride at Hyde Park Stables. Five miles of trails wind through the park, allowing visitors to combine horseback riding with sightseeing. No previous riding experience is required, and children over age five are welcome. The stables provide riding helmets. There is a weight limit of thirteen stone for riders. Thirteen *stone*? That is about 180 pounds or 80 kilograms. For more information visit the stable's website at www.hydeparkstables.com

The cost of a horseback ride through the park is very expensive. A better alternative? Rent a bicycle from London's nearby cycle hire stations and ride along one of the park's designated bike routes. Spend an hour or an afternoon.

During the summer, Hyde Park often hosts concerts and other large-scale events. Hyde Park also holds a huge winter fair that is a popular family holiday celebration. It pays to check the park's events listings if you want to attend an event.

Admission to Hyde Park and Kensington Gardens is free. There are cafés, restaurants, snack bars, and plenty of picnic spots. Toilets can be found in several locations. Most areas of the parks are wheelchair accessible and there is a shuttle service for the mobility impaired.

Website: www.royalparks.org.uk

Coram's Fields

Not far from the British Museum, a seven-acre play area sits on the site of one of London's first charities to help children. The old Foundling Hospital is long gone, although the nearby Foundling Museum is worth a visit (website: www.foundlingmuseum.org.uk).

In the hospital's place is Coram's Fields—a large park incorporating playgrounds, a community center, and a small city farm. Many of the activities here are geared to local residents, but visiting children are welcome to explore. This is one of the best children's parks in the area, with a large sand pit, swings, and seesaws for younger kids. Older children can try out a zip line and tunnel slide. There is age-appropriate climbing equipment for all. The park is only open to children under age sixteen and adults without children are not admitted. There is a café and a picnic area. Toilets and baby changing areas are available in two locations.

Website: www.coramsfields.org

A Garden In the Sky

Undoubtedly the highest garden in the city, the Sky Garden offers some of London's best views. Perched at the top of the modern "walkie talkie" office tower at 20 Fenchurch Street, the garden is a quasi-public space. That means you can visit, but only with advance tickets, at limited times, and after an undergoing an airport-style security search. Still, the 360-degree view and expansive indoor landscaping is worth the effort. There are also several restaurants and bars onsite.

Website: www.skygarden.london

Regent's Park

The largest park in downtown London is located on the northern border of the city center. Regent's Park, like many others, began its life as royal hunting grounds during the reign of Henry VIII. John Nash designed the park landscaping in the early 1800s. Who was John Nash? He designed Buckingham Palace, Regent's Canal, the wide-open space of Piccadilly Circus and curving Regent's Street, the Royal Mews, Marble Arch...the list seems endless.

There's a little of everything here. Regent's Park is sports oriented, with a running track, athletic fields, and—surprisingly—American softball fields. A stroll north lands you at the London Zoo. During warm months, the scent of roses wafts from Queen Mary's Garden at the center of the park. In the summer, Regent's Park hosts an open-air theater featuring Shakespeare and other popular productions. There is also a children's boating pond where kids can captain small paddleboats. And yes, Regent's Park has playgrounds (four of them).

The park has cafés, restaurants, snack bars, and plenty of picnic spots. There are toilets in several locations and most areas of the park are wheelchair accessible.

Website: www.royalparks.org.uk

Hampstead Heath

Let's go fly a kite

Up to the highest height!

Let's go fly a kite and send it soaring

Up through the atmosphere

Up where the air is clear

Oh, let's go fly a kite!

—*Mary Poppins* words and music by Richard M. Sherman and Robert B. Sherman

Hampstead Heath is an oasis of open space just four miles from the hustle and bustle of central London. Hampstead, the village that adjoins the heath, is an upscale neighborhood featuring some of London's most expensive residential real estate.

Visiting the 790-acre heath is like stepping through a portal into the green countryside of England. You can see London—the views of the city are incredible—but you can barely hear it. What you will hear in Hampstead Heath is music from a summertime concert on the grounds of historic Kenwood House, joggers puffing their way along pathways, or the squeal of kite-flying children.

Did we say kite flying? The musical *Mary Poppins* (1964) concludes with the once-troubled Banks family happily flying a kite in Hampstead (or a least the Hollywood sound stage version). Another Poppins-related site in Hampstead is the Admiral's House, where fictional Admiral Boom fires a cannon from his rooftop every day. Mary Shepard, illustrator of the original Mary Poppins book series, lived in Hampstead and took many inspirations from the area, as did author P. L. Travers.

Historic Kenwood House sits majestically on a ridge in the middle

of Hampstead Heath. This great house is compact enough to tour in less than an hour and there are explorer backpacks and activities for children. The grounds of Kenwood will look familiar to fans of the iconic London film *Notting Hill* (1999). Curiously, *Belle* (2014), is a film about one of Kenwood's famous residents, but the movie was filmed elsewhere. Kenwood House, Hampstead Heath, and Hampstead village all reprise to "star" in the film *Hampstead* (2017).

Hampstead Heath offers swimming and fishing ponds, playgrounds, bandstands, and even a small zoo. If your children want to fly a kite, or just run off some pent-up energy, Hampstead Heath is the perfect spot.

There are cafés at Parliament Hill and Golders Hill, and a restaurant at Kenwood House. Public toilets are available in several locations. Many pathways and areas of Hampstead Heath are wheelchair accessible.

Website: www.cityoflondon.gov.uk/hampsteadheath

Jurassic Park

Are your children fascinated with dinosaurs? Today's little dinosaur experts can easily identify and rattle off facts about a T-Rex or Stegosaurus. But in the mid-1800s, dinosaurs were a novelty. Almost nobody knew much about them, and even paleontologists were prone to imaginative speculation. Thirty life-sized "best guess" dino sculptures were installed in Crystal Palace Park between 1853 and 1855.

Bring your kids and come roam with the dinosaurs, then explore more of Crystal Palace Park's 200 acres. There is a children's play area and city farm with live animals, a fishing lake and even a small maze.

Many areas of Crystal Palace Park are wheelchair accessible. There are toilets near the park visitor's center and a café near the dinosaurs.

Websites: www.bromley.gov.uk/crystalpalacepark
　　　　　 www.cpdinosaurs.org

Visit the Parks After Dark?

In England, there was scarcely an amount of order and protection to justify much national boasting. Daring burglaries by armed men, and highway robberies, took place in the capital itself every night.

—*A Tale of Two Cities* by Charles Dickens

Based on Charles Dickens' description, London street crime was a real problem in 1775. Although today's streetwise travelers generally avoid city parks after dark, London's central parks still feel relatively safe, even at night. The most threatening sights we've seen during evening walks in St. James's and Green Parks were the guards on patrol near a royal residence. We rounded a corner and faced two camouflaged soldiers carrying automatic weapons! Although many parks officially close in the evenings, their pathways are used by late-night urban strollers. Normal precautions apply.

Go Cruising

Believe me, my young friend, there is nothing—
absolutely nothing—half so much worth doing
as simply messing about in boats.

—*The Wind in the Willows* by Kenneth Grahame

Crisscrossed by rivers and canals, London is an ideal place to take a family cruise. Choices include a riverboat on the Thames, a unique amphibious tour, an adrenaline-inducing speedboat ride, a sedate canal boat on Regent's Canal, and a cruise (actually more of a "spin") on the London Eye.

River Cruises

Taking a boat ride in London can serve many purposes:

- The water view provides a unique perspective of many famous sites.
- Sometimes a boat is the most logical way to get to where you're going.
- The phrase "Hey, kids, let's go on a boat trip!" is usually received with more enthusiasm than "Hey, kids, let's go into this cathedral!"

Boating on the Thames is a practical and fun way to reach several destinations from central London: downriver to Greenwich, Canary Wharf, and the Thames River flood barrier; upriver to Richmond, Kew, and Hampton Court; or just sightseeing between Tower Bridge and Westminster. Transport for London operates or coordinates most river services. There has been a concerted effort to expand the use of the Thames by commuters as well as pleasure cruisers, and the Transport for London website lists a dizzying array of boat routes.

Before taking a cruise to someplace like Hampton Court, decide how much time you want to spend on a boat—Hampton is a four-hour boat ride from London. The Thames loops and turns, so river trips can take much longer than other modes of transportation. On a more manageable scale, visitors can take fifty-minute sightseeing cruises from several London river piers.

The least expensive cruises are short jaunts on the River Bus commuter boat routes. More expensive evening cruises feature (often mediocre) champagne, food, and entertainment. Larger boats have food concessions, toilets, and other facilities. Most boats are wheelchair accessible.

Website: www.tfl.gov.uk (look for the "River" section)

Hop Aboard the Duck

Can't decide whether to take a bus tour on London's streets or a boat

tour on the Thames? You can do both on a DUKW. These craft started out as World War II amphibious vehicles, capable of wading through rivers and driving overland. Refitted and painted bright yellow, these strange-looking hybrids take visitors on a driving tour through central London before splashing down into the Thames. Yes, the bright yellow DUKWs look out of place rumbling past Big Ben. But that won't faze most children. The Duck Tour is a big hit with many visiting families.

Be aware, DUKWs have no onboard facilities and are not wheelchair accessible. Tours leave from Belvedere Road, next to Jubilee Gardens near the London Eye.

Website: www.londonducktours.co.uk

The Need For Speed?

The fastest way to experience the Thames has to be aboard a high-speed Rib Tour or Thames Jet. These speedboats provide a James Bond-worthy thrill ride on the river. It's not for the fainthearted. Rib Tour boats depart from Festival Pier, about one-quarter mile downriver from the London Eye. Thames Jet boats leave from Westminster Pier, directly across the river from the Eye.

Websites: www.ribtourslondon.com
            www.thamesjet.com

Boating Along Regent's Canal

There is no better way to get to the London Zoo than to cruise on a boat up or down Regent's Canal. Of course, you don't have to stop and see the animals at the zoo; canal cruises are just a great way to relax and get off the beaten path. There are a few interesting regency buildings, iron bridges, and tunnels along the way. At one time, London's canals connected the city's manufacturing centers before railways took over.

Regent's Canal boat trips travel between Little Venice and Camden Town. Little Venice is home to waterside cafés, pubs, and eateries. Camden Town is best known for its alternative culture, international

markets, and music venues. The London Waterbus operates one-way or round-trip service between Camden Lock and Little Venice and also stops at the London Zoo. Jason's Trips provides a round-trip sightseeing cruise starting at Little Venice. The Jenny Wren sightseeing cruises start and end near Camden Lock.

Canal boats have no onboard facilities and wheelchair accessibility is limited.

Websites: www.jasons.co.uk
www.londonwaterbus.com
www.walkersquay.com (Jenny Wren)

A Towpath Stroll

If you choose to walk along the Regent's Canal towpath you can visit the new urban landscape at King's Cross. Once a wasteland, now a playground, today's King's Cross is a poster child for London redevelopment. Upscale retail and tech-centric office buildings spring like modernistic mushrooms in the area around, over, and under King's Cross and St. Pancras rail stations. Busy bars and concept restaurants abound, drawing office workers, tourists and arts students from the nearby campus of Central St. Martins College.

Is there any refuge from the bustle? A place to slow down, turn off the smartphone and escape the burgeoning modernity of Kings Cross? Actually, yes. A few pockets of passivity can be found along Regent's Canal within a short stroll—watch out for the Segway tourists!—of Kings Cross station.

Don't miss **Word on the Water**, a floating independent bookstore moored on the canal towpath just north of Kings Cross station. Step aboard, say hello to the lounging store dog, and explore the books packed bow-to-stern in this converted canal boat. There's a nice selection of children's books here.

Wedged between the canal and the St. Pancras Station rail yards, **Camley Street Natural Park** is a tiny slice of nature rescued from an industrial wasteland. The diminutive nature reserve has woodland, grassland and wetland habitats populated by birds, insects, and

plant life. The visitor's center is great for kids. For information, see the park's website at www.wildlondon.org.uk (search under "nature reserves").

Finally, escape the modern redevelopment landscape with a stroll through leafy **St. Pancras Gardens** and a peek inside St. Pancras Old Church. The gardens were created from the church graveyard. The gardens and church are on the west side of the rail yards, a few hundred steps from Camley Street Natural Park. Redevelopment pressure of an earlier age caused most of the graves to be relocated or paved over during construction of St. Pancras Rail Station. The macabre task of exhuming the dead fell to poet Thomas Hardy who served as a rail station architectural assistant. Hardy's poem "The Levelled Churchyard" reminds rail patrons:

O passenger, pray list and catch
Our sighs and piteous groans,
Half stifled in this jumbled patch
Of wrenched memorial stones!

The so-called Hardy Tree behind the church is surrounded with stacked abandoned tombstones. Gruesome? Yes, but fascinating nevertheless.

The London Eye

My favorite thing to do in London is to fly the Eye.... On a clear day you can see for twenty-five miles in all directions....It takes thirty minutes to go full circle. And then your capsule goes lower and you are sad because you do not want the ride to end. You would like to go round one more time, but it's not allowed. So you get out feeling like an astronaut coming down from space, a little lighter than you were.

—*The London Eye Mystery* by Siobhan Dowd

It's hard to miss the giant Ferris wheel across the river from Big Ben and Parliament. The London Eye's operators insist that their commercial venture is an "observation wheel," not a Ferris wheel, but that distinction is lost on some visitors.

Terminology aside, the London Eye is a fantastic vantage point from which to view downtown London. Visitors ride in large observation pods that slowly rotate around the 450-foot-tall wheel. The combination of the slow motion and the enclosed pods makes for a tame ride. Visibility is up to twenty-five miles, so on a clear day you can't see forever, but you might see as far as the town of Windsor. Riding the London Eye at sunset on a clear or partly cloudy day is an unforgettable London experience. During busy summer months, lines can be long at this popular attraction. Advance booking is a good idea.

There are cafés, toilets and baby changing areas at the Eye's ticket office. The London Eye is wheelchair accessible.

Website: www.londoneye.com

Do a Brass Rubbing at St. Martin-in-the-Fields

If the weather turns nasty during a visit to London—and it may—doing a brass rubbing is a fun rainy-day activity for families. The tradition started with rubbings on the ancient burial vault brasses of knights and nobility, done on paper using chalk or charcoal. Eventually, all that rubbing began to threaten the survival of the brasses, so copies were cast. Brass rubbing centers have large selections of brass casts. Kids can choose to copy knights, ladies, dragons, or other medieval brasses.

Here's the process. Start by taping a large piece of rubbing paper to the face of the brass plate, then carefully rub across the paper with a special colored rubbing crayon. It's similar to putting a piece of paper on top of a coin and rubbing it with a pencil. Seemingly endless rubbing with the crayon produces a two-dimensional copy of the brass. The rubbing center staff will roll up the completed work and place it in a cardboard tube. The best thing about this souvenir is that you made it yourself!

Brass rubbing is a good activity for artistically inclined children from about age seven and up. It takes a while to satisfactorily complete a brass rubbing, so plan at least thirty minutes to an hour or more, depending on your skill, persistence, and the size of the brass on which you are working.

London's brass rubbing center is at St. Martin-in-the-Fields Church just off Trafalgar Square. St. Martin's has a cafeteria where hungry brass rubbers can get a quick meal. The cafeteria floor is partially made of stone slabs that mark the burial places of former church members. It's not as macabre as it sounds. After repeated exposure to England's innumerable abbeys, cathedrals, and churches, children become accustomed to walking over the not-so-recently departed.

The St. Martin's cafeteria is fast and convenient and provides a lot of reasonably priced choices.

While you are here, go upstairs and take a look at the rest of St. Martin-in-the-Fields Church. St. Martin's is home to frequent lunchtime musical recitals. These are relatively brief, informal concerts that most children can sit through with minimal squirming. It's a chance for families to absorb some London culture in a palatable dose. The lunchtime concerts are free, but there is a collection bin at the door.

St. Martin's is renowned for its music programs. Adults and older children can enjoy the church's frequent evening candlelight concerts, and St. Martin's crypt is converted into an atmospheric jazz venue on select Wednesday nights.

The site has toilets and baby changing areas and is wheelchair accessible.

Website: www.stmartin-in-the-fields.org

Go Shopping—Do
We Have To?

Then, one day, James' mother and father went to London
to do some shopping, and there a terrible thing happened.
Both of them suddenly got eaten up (in full daylight, mind
you, and on a crowded street) by an enormous angry
rhinoceros which had escaped from the London Zoo.

—*James and the Giant Peach* by Roald Dahl

Rhinos are rare in London, so you are unlikely to meet the same fate
as James's parents. But your children may still resist going shopping.

And there are some good reasons not to shop during your London vacation:

- London can be an expensive place to shop.
- The value added tax can make things even more expensive.
- You can buy much of the same merchandise back home or online.

Here is another reason to minimize shopping. You are on a visit to a world-class city, you've spent a lot of money to get here, and London offers all kinds of exciting, unique experiences. So why use valuable vacation time shopping?

But there is one shopping stop that children will definitely enjoy: **Hamley's Toy Store**. This is no mere toyshop. Hamley's is a huge, high-quality toy department store on Regent Street. Founded in 1760 and opened in its current location in 1881, Hamley's has seven floors of toys to entice young shoppers and their parents. For information, see Hamley's website at www.hamleys.com

Elegant, curving **Regent Street** is home to a host of major stores. Many are unique to London, but some you might find in your hometown. All are expensive. Walk north and you come to **Oxford Street**, which overflows with shopping options, including John Lewis, Selfridges, and Marks and Spenser department stores. At times, Oxford Street and Regent Street are wall-to-curb with shopping crowds.

If your philosophy is "I shop, therefore, I am," you won't be disappointed by **Harrods** in Knightsbridge. But dragging a child through this massive, upscale department store can be torturous. On the plus side, Harrods does have a toy area (although it certainly can't rival Hamley's). Harrods boasts an enormous food hall and walking through it is a gastronomic event for the whole family. If you pass by Harrods at night, your kids may think that the store is decorated for Christmas because the building is outlined by thousands of tiny lights. Unlike many department stores, Harrods has just two major sales, in July and January, and these events attract throngs of bargain hunters.

By contrast, **Fortnum & Mason** on Piccadilly street in Mayfair offers shopping on a scale that most people can manage—if their wallets can take it. The high-end store is impressive. Our children remarked that

Fortnum & Mason was the only place where they bought cookies from a salesperson wearing a tuxedo. The basement and ground floor food departments are filled with teas, jams, biscuits, and other delicacies. Alas, there's no toy department.

While you are in the Mayfair area, take a walk through **Burlington Arcade**. You will discover that the shopping mall is not a new phenomenon. The ornate covered arcade was built in 1819 and today it is occupied by a series of upscale shops. The security guards here look a little different than those at home. With their top hats and formal uniforms, Burlington Arcade's beadles are a combination security guard and information guide. Piccadilly Arcade, right across the street, opened in 1910, so it's a relative retail newcomer.

London's prime shopping venues aren't all historic. If your children resist going on a shopping trip, then London's massive Westfield Shopping Centre has the answer: drop them off at **Kidzania**. This is an indoor mini-city where kids can take on the role of a doctor, a dentist, a firefighter, an actor or other adult occupation. It's more than simple dress up. Kidzania has sixty themed activities staged throughout elaborate interactive areas. Located just west of Notting Hill, Kidzania

allows parents to drop off children (over age eight) for up to four hours of supervised activities. Bottom line for many kids? It's a lot more fun than four hours in a shopping mall. See the Kidzania website at www.kidzania.co.uk

There are many **bookstores** scattered throughout London, some selling new editions and some offering antiquarian books. Visiting children can learn what British kids are reading. Adults can look for first editions of great English works, although a first edition of a Dickens novel would be a rather expensive souvenir. Some of the booksellers operate crowded, dusty shops filled floor-to-ceiling with antique books.

London's street markets and traditional food markets offer a glimpse of shopping as it existed before big-box stores and online retail. Depending on their interests and tolerance for browsing, children may enjoy strolling through street markets. London's old-style food markets are also dramatically different from modern grocery stores.

One of the better-known markets consists of antiques and flea market stalls snaking along **Portobello Road**. The market's popularity

peaks on Saturdays when it can be dauntingly crowded. Hint: market tourists stream north from Notting Hill Gate Underground station, but you're better off starting from Ladbroke Grove station and walking south.

Camden claims to be the world's largest antiques market—perhaps a frightening factoid for children. **Camden Market**, northeast of Regent's Park, is filled with flea markets and stores offering quirky goods. Camden has open-air market stalls and storefront shops that generally operate seven days a week.

For traditional covered food markets, head to beautiful **Leadenhall Market**, located in London's financial district. There's a family film bonus waiting here: Leadenhall was a filming location for some Diagon Alley scenes in the Harry Potter films.

Greenwich offers a smallish antiques and crafts market. And **Borough Market** is a bustling food market at London Bridge. This is just a sampling of the many markets throughout London.

Exit through the gift shop? Don't overlook the shops in museums and visitor attractions. The Transport Museum in Covent Garden is filled with unique souvenirs featuring popular London Transport graphics. The Tower of London's shops have lots of items for children.

While **museum shops** are not immune to tacky, cheap souvenirs, they do offer books and reproduction items that usually cannot be found elsewhere. One of our favorites is the compact shop at the Courtauld Gallery art museum.

The **Covent Garden** and **Seven Dials** areas abound in specialty shops. Kids will enjoy stores here that specialize in kites, skates, cartoon art, and toys. The small streets and alleyways north and west of the Covent Garden piazza and marketplace house a variety of independent shops.

Wherever adults choose to shop in London, they can count on free advice from children.

"The Toy Department," Michael reminded her, "is in that direction." "I know thank you. Don't point," [Mary Poppins] said, and paid her bill with aggravating slowness.

—*Mary Poppins* by P. L. Travers

Go to the Theater

*The theatre was quite full and Paddington waved
to the people down below. Much to Mrs. Brown's
embarrassment, several of them pointed and waved back.*

— *A Bear Called Paddington* by Michael Bond

London's West End theater district offers a vast array of shows, but finding something appropriate for younger children can be a challenge. Musicals are often a good bet if you choose wisely: *School of Rock*, not *The Woman in Black*; *The Lion King*, not *King Lear*. Okay, *King Lear* isn't a musical, but you get the idea.

The Internet is a great resource for choosing shows. The Society of London Theatre's website (www.officiallondontheatre.com) is, as the name implies, the "official" guide to London theater. The society also operates TKTS, the legitimate discount ticket booth in Leicester Square. The commercial What's On Stage site (website: www.whatsonstage.com) has listings for performing arts events throughout Britain. Users can search for events by location, date, or type of performance. Both websites include theater reviews, seating charts, and a way to order tickets, albeit with hefty booking fees. After arriving in London, visitors can pick up copies of guides like *Time Out London* for more theater information.

Most of London's major theaters are located in the West End theater district close to Piccadilly Circus or Leicester Square. There is another group in the Covent Garden area. Because London's museums and tourist attractions usually close by 6:00 p.m., an evening theater performance works well for many visitors. As a bonus, the theater is a chance to sit down after walking all day. Those who don't mind walking a bit more can use the Underground to get to most theaters, but a taxi will drop you right at the lobby door.

Getting a taxi or hailing a ride after the performance can be a challenge because all shows end at about the same time, and competition for rides is fierce. The area around Leicester Square, including the Tube stop, is often very crowded with a mixture of theater patrons and a slightly rowdy bar crowd on Friday and Saturday nights. Extra vigilance is advisable.

How to Get Tickets

Online ticket agencies sell London theater tickets, but most charge substantial service fees. Overseas travelers can sometimes order tickets directly from theater websites or box offices. Booking through the box office is often less expensive than using a ticket agent. Keep in mind that many theaters have exclusive marketing deals with commercial ticket agencies that you probably won't be able to bypass.

What about discounted theater tickets? Although standing in line at a ticket outlet hardly constitutes family fun, it can save you money. Many tickets are half price plus a small fee. One drawback is that families traveling together need seats together, and these can be hard to find at the bargain outlet. Another problem with the ticket outlet is the limited selection of shows, because the most popular productions don't need to discount tickets. Be wary of using anyplace other than the official TKTS ticket office in Leicester Square (website: www.tkts.co.uk). Watch out for ticket touts (scalpers) who ply the Leicester Square area and can charge exorbitant rates for subpar seats.

One obvious way to get tickets is simply to walk up to the theater box office on the day of the show and see what is available. Theaters occasionally have unsold and returned tickets even for popular productions. Finally, if you are desperate to see a popular show and you are staying in an upscale hotel, check with the concierge. A good concierge can sometimes make rare tickets appear as if by magic—for the right price.

The Globe Theatre

All the world's a stage,

And all the men and women merely players.

—*As You Like It* by William Shakespeare

Because theater thrives in modern London, it is hard to imagine a time when playwrights and actors struggled against religious

and government suppression. But the famed Globe Theatre was once forced to relocate to the south bank of the Thames to escape the unfriendly atmosphere in the City of London. In 1597, after an unsympathetic landlord raised the land rent, the theater company moved the Globe—piece by piece—from its City location to Southwark.

In 1613, the Globe Theatre burned to the ground, allegedly the result of a cannon shot during a performance of the play *Henry VIII*. A new theater was built on the site, but it lasted only until 1642, when those fun-loving Puritans forced it to close. The Globe was torn down in 1644, and the site was virtually forgotten. It was not until the 1980s that the foundation of the theater was discovered. The remains of the original Globe are buried below a newer (but still historic) building that was constructed on the site.

What Globe visitors see today is a nearby reconstruction begun under the leadership of the late Sam Wanamaker, an American actor and film director. But to call the Globe a reconstruction is to sell it short. The new Globe was painstakingly completed using authentic Elizabethan building techniques, and the result is both a theater and a tourist attraction. In 2014 a new indoor theater opened adjacent to the Globe. The Sam Wanamaker Playhouse is another stunning re-creation—a beautiful 340-seat Jacobean theater. Amazingly, productions in this new space are staged in candlelight.

If your children cannot sit still for a full-fledged Shakespearean production, at least take the building tour of the legendary theater and a quick look at the adjoining Globe Exhibition.

The Globe has a restaurant, two bars and a café (no outside food allowed). Toilets and baby changing areas are available. Some areas of the theater are not wheelchair accessible.

Website: www.shakespearesglobe.com

Unicorn Theatre

Many theaters offer occasional programs and performances for children, but the Unicorn is a bit more focused. This is a theater built and operated specifically for kids. The Unicorn is located in Southwark, not far from Tower Bridge. The Unicorn offers theater-related activities and a changing lineup of performances, helpfully graded by "size":

* XS for children from birth to age four
* S for kids from four to seven
* M for kids age seven through twelve
* L for children thirteen and over
* And the occasional XL for adults

There is a snack bar onsite, plus toilets and baby changing areas. The theater is wheelchair accessible.

Website: www.unicorntheatre.com

Puppets on the Water

London has a long history of puppetry, but puppet theater is scarce in the twenty-first century. That's what makes the Puppet Theatre Barge so unique—live puppet theater staged in a converted river barge. Since the theater floats, it is able to rotate seasonally between Little Venice on Regent's Canal in central London, and the Thames riverside in suburban Richmond. Shows last about an hour, refreshments are available and there is a toilet onboard. The barge is not wheelchair accessible.

Website: www.puppetbarge.com

Start Rambling

Where am I going? I don't quite know.
Down to the stream where the king-cups grow—
Up on the hill where the pine-trees blow—
Anywhere, anywhere. I don't know.
—"Spring Morning" by A. A. Milne

Britain is a country of walkers, or "ramblers" in Britspeak. Unlike in some parts of the world, where private property paranoia keeps walkers from roaming freely, hikers have the right to trek through much of the British countryside. There are more than 140,000 miles of public footpaths and rights-of-way in England and Wales—amazing considering the small size of these countries. British hikers refer to themselves as ramblers with good reason, because they truly ramble across the land. Hiking enthusiasts banded together to form the Ramblers Association. The group's website (www.ramblers.org.uk) is a good starting point for anyone interested in walking in Britain.

The detailed instructions contained in British walking guides can be fun for children to decipher. Arm your kids with trail guides that describe walks using phrases like "go over the stile, turn right at the large oak tree, past the stone wall on your left . . ." Once kids learn that stiles are fence or wall crossings, they are ready for an adventure on the trail.

Wherever you ramble in Britain, look for information on local walking trails. There is no better way to see the country and get beyond the normal tourist routes. For example, while touring the Cotswolds, we were dismayed when we arrived at Bourton-on-the-Water. The tour books had described a pretty, rural town. The reality of Bourton-on-the-Water on a midsummer day was dozens of tour buses and hordes of visitors. Luckily we were carrying a book detailing off-the-beaten-path walks throughout the country. Using that guide, we went over stiles, through fields, and around cows to tiny Wyck Rissington—a village two miles and centuries removed from Bourton. Wyck Rissington is the quietest village imaginable, with few tourists and no souvenir shops. We ate a Father's Day picnic in an ancient churchyard, then spent a few minutes visiting the village church. A two-mile hike had taken us from the tourist version of the Cotswolds to the real thing.

But hiking is not limited to rural Britain. The Thames Path winds 180 miles from the river's source in rural Gloucestershire to the Thames Barrier below Greenwich. In the process, the path runs through Windsor, Hampton Court, and downtown London.

Walking The Mall

Strictly speaking, there are not many hiking trails in town, but London is very much a city for walkers. The Mall—one of the widest and most historic boulevards in London—is closed to vehicles on Sundays so that pedestrians can stroll unimpeded. Before walking here, make sure kids know that the Mall in London isn't home to hundreds of stores and a food court. The Mall is the wide street leading from Buckingham Palace along St. James's Park toward Whitehall and the Admiralty Arch. This is one of the most famous parade routes in London, and you can make your own parade on any Sunday. Properly pronounced, *Mall* rhymes with the word *shall*. And to add to the confusion, there are two parallel streets here: the Mall, and Pall Mall, which is a busy street just a few hundred feet north. Pedestrians can safely stroll down the Mall on Sunday. If you try this on Pall Mall, you will get run over.

Walking in London does present some hazards, primarily when crossing streets. Tourists from most other countries generally look left for oncoming traffic, but because Britons drive on the left, an unwitting tourist may never see the lorry (truck) coming from the right. Smack! One less repeat visitor. Seriously, the only good defensive strategy is to swivel your head when crossing a street in London. Look right, look left, then look right and left again. That way your instincts won't get you killed. Recognizing the potential hazard, London traffic officials have painted the words "look right" or "look left" on the pavement at some pedestrian crossings.

London crosswalks come in several varieties. Zebra crossings have painted stripes on the pavement, where all traffic should stop for pedestrians. Zebra-stripe crossings are usually further marked by curbside light poles with round, blinking globes to remind drivers to stop for pedestrians. X crossings—also known as pedestrian scrambles—have signals to stop all traffic at busy intersections and allow pedestrians to cross diagonally. Pelicans and Puffins are crossings where walkers must wait for a signal to cross. Traffic islands are mid-road safety areas for pedestrians where there is no actual crosswalk and vehicles are not required to stop.

Walking the Wall

Assuming you survive crossing the streets, you can take a walk that traces the outlines of the old wall that surrounded Londinium, the Roman precursor to London. This is a one-and-a-half mile walk between the Tower of London and Aldersgate Street, with twenty-one historical markers and a few glimpses of the old wall along the way. It's a good walk to combine with a visit to the Museum of London.

Walking Around the Palace

If the weather is good, visitors flock to Buckingham Palace to see the changing of the guard. And while that is a quintessential tourist activity, a walk in and around nearby St. James's Park is a relaxing contrast. St. James's Park is conveniently close to an amazing array of historic locations: Westminster Abbey, St. James's Palace, the Churchill War Rooms, Number 10 Downing Street, Horse Guards Parade, Scotland Yard—and did we mention Buckingham Palace?

Walking the Riverbank

Another pleasant walk covers the South Bank, generally following the Thames Path from Westminster Bridge downstream to Tower Bridge. Attractions abound along the river in South Bank. The area offers spectacular views across the water toward the historic monuments of central London, including Parliament, Whitehall, St. Paul's Cathedral, and the Tower of London. The Westminster-to-Tower Bridge route is a great walk to take in conjunction with visits to the Florence Nightingale Museum, the London Eye, the Tate Modern, the Millennium Bridge, the Globe Theatre, the HMS Belfast, and Tower Bridge.

Strolling downstream along the south bank of the river, you will also pass Gabriel's Wharf, a festival marketplace with shops, bars, and restaurants. Hungry families can seek out the local gourmet pizza place here or grab some takeout food to eat outside and enjoy great views across the river. Some of the shops in Gabriel's Wharf sell locally designed and produced goods.

Not far past Gabriel's Wharf is the distinctive Oxo Tower. At one time, the south bank of the Thames was lined with power-generating stations. You will see them upstream at Battersea and further downstream at the Tate Modern. In its original incarnation, the Oxo Tower complex was one of these riverside power plants. But the site was rebuilt during the late 1920s, adding with the art deco tower. The letters O-X-O? Sneaky advertising for the Oxo brand of beef stock cubes that were made here. The letters are windows placed to spell out the brand name after local government authorities denied the company's request to erect huge illuminated signs. The Oxo Tower complex was redeveloped in the 1990s as residential and commercial space. The tower houses an upscale restaurant, bistro, and bar boasting some of the best views in London, with outdoor seating overlooking the Thames.

A bit further downstream at the Tate Modern Museum you arrive at Millennium Bridge, which was destroyed in the film version of *Harry Potter and the Half-Blood Prince*. Although that event never happened

in real life, the bridge did experience some rough times soon after it opened in 2000. The modern pedestrian bridge swayed alarmingly in the wind, earning it the nickname the Wobbly Bridge and causing engineers to scramble to reinforce the structure. The bridge has stood firmly since.

For better or worse, modern buildings have sprouted like mushrooms across central London, and many of them are visible along this walk. They have taken on peculiar names like the Gerkin, Cheesegrater, Shard, and Darth Vader's Helmet. No doubt your kids can come up with their own names for these modern edifices. Darth Vader's Helmet is the headquarters of the Greater London Authority, just downstream from the HMS Belfast. This is London's city hall.

For one of the best views of London, head for the top of the Shard. This modern pyramid is near Southwark Cathedral. The View from the Shard gives visitors a 360-degree panorama on its two main observation decks—one enclosed at level sixty-nine, and one partially open to the skies on level seventy-two.

Walking With a Guide

If you want to combine walking with a guided tour, several companies offer walking tours. London Walks (website: www.walks.com) is one of the best-known walking tour companies in London. Walks usually focus on an area of the city or a historical theme and are led by guides who are both personable and knowledgeable. Walks generally last two hours and are very affordable. Evening walks featuring Jack the Ripper, ghosts, or pub-crawls may not be appropriate for all children. We have found only one downside to signing up for a guided walk. By the time the tour starts, you may already have walked so much on your own that you will be too tired to go.

Find the Wild Kingdom

It was a very sunny Saturday and the zoo was crowded with families. The Dursleys bought Dudley and Piers large chocolate ice creams at the entrance and then, because the smiling lady in the van had asked Harry what he wanted before they could hurry him away, they bought him a cheap lemon ice pop. It wasn't bad, either, Harry thought, licking it as they watched a gorilla scratching its head who looked remarkably like Dudley, except that it wasn't blond.

—*Harry Potter and the Philosopher's Stone* by J. K. Rowling

London Zoo

London is hardly a prime travel destination for wildlife seekers. Yes, there are pigeons in Trafalgar Square, exotic waterfowl in St. James's Park, and even urban-adapted foxes wandering parts of the city. But most London animals tend to be of the captive variety, and the best spot for observing animal wildlife in London is the zoo in Regent's Park. The London Zoo may not meet all your criteria for a must-see tourist attraction, especially if you have visited world-class zoos in other cities. But if you are traveling with children, the London Zoo may be on your itinerary.

In 1914, at the start of World War I, a Canadian army officer gave the zoo an American black bear named Winnie. Two zoo visitors, writer A. A. Milne and his son Christopher, transformed the bear into a children's literary classic. Winnie and many other famous zoo residents are history now, and the London Zoo has reinvented itself with a modern theme of "conservation in action." Even with this lofty mission, the zoo knows that visitors want to see cute, playful animals. When sloth bears were reintroduced to the outdoor exhibits, the bears became the zoo's poster children.

Operating since 1828, the Regent's Park site is one of the oldest zoos in the world. Zoo highlights include a walk-through lemur area and a beach and pool for the zoo's penguin colony. In the Rainforest Life exhibit, tropical animals bask, and Londoners swelter, in a constant 80° F humid heat. The zoo's old aquarium exhibit can be disappointing for anyone who has visited London's modern aquarium at County Hall. But keep in mind that London Zoo had the world's first public aquarium.

"I want to show you llama poop," said the four-year-old boy to his father. The Animal Adventure children's zoo and playground is a highlight of the London Zoo because children can interact with the animals here. Kids can observe animals living in the Treetop Zone and the Roots Zone. Venture to the Splash Zone for some watery play and to the Touch Zone to pet and feed pigs, sheep, goats, and donkeys.

If you *belong* in a zoo, the London Zoo offers one more experience that might tempt visiting families—stay overnight in the zoo's Gir Lion Lodges. This is London lodging like no other. Visitors spend the night in small cottages within earshot of the zoo's lion enclosures. The packages include drinks, dinner, breakfast, and after-hours zoo tours. No, the zoo does not employ chimpanzees as bellhops or penguins as waiters.

The London Zoo covers thirty-six acres in the northern corner of Regent's Park and is bisected by Regent's Canal. The zoo has cafés, snack bars, and outdoor picnic sites. Toilets and baby changing areas are available. Limited areas of the zoo are not wheelchair accessible.

Website: www.londonzoo.co.uk

Something Fishy on the Thames

London boasts a modern aquarium on the south bank of the Thames within walking distance of Big Ben. The Old County Hall, formerly a city hall for London area governments, has been converted into hotels, shops, the London Dungeon, and the world-class London Aquarium.

With its multimillion-liter tanks, the Sea Life London Aquarium is one of Britain's largest, and it rivals US aquariums in Boston, Baltimore, or Long Beach. The aquarium is home to thousands of sea critters, including some that kids can touch. A coral reef exhibit combines aquatic specimens with interactive audiovisual presentations. Most children will enjoy the rain forest experience, the piranhas in the tropical exhibit, and the sharks in the Pacific Ocean tank. Want to get

even closer to the sharks? The aquarium offers shark feeding and a snorkeling-with-the-sharks experience. Hopefully, these are separate events.

The aquarium has toilets and baby changing areas on every level and the site is fully wheelchair accessible. There is no coat/package check.

Website: www.visitsealife.com/london

And Something Fowl

Just over three miles west—as the duck flies—from Buckingham Palace, London's wildfowl make themselves at home in the London Wetland Centre. Located on the site of an abandoned waterworks, one hundred acres of wetlands creates a habitat that attracts wildlife and human visitors alike.

The staff has counted some 180 wild bird species here. The Wetland Centre is not a top tourist destination, but it is popular with local school groups and nature lovers. The education center and its displays will interest budding naturalists. Be sure and check for daily walks and special events as part of your visit.

There is a restaurant onsite. Toilets and baby changing areas are available. The Wetland Centre is wheelchair accessible.

Website: www.wwt.org.uk (select the London location)

Watch the Changing of the Guard

They're changing the guard at Buckingham Palace—
Christopher Robin went down with Alice.
We saw a guard in a sentry-box.
"One of the sergeants looks after their socks," Says Alice.
They're changing the guard at Buckingham Palace—
Christopher Robin went down with Alice. They've
great big parties inside the grounds.
"I wouldn't be King for a hundred pounds," Says Alice.
—"Buckingham Palace" by A. A. Milne

What tourist visits London without witnessing the changing of the guard? Some do, of course, but we suspect that almost none of them are touring with kids. Thankfully, there are more ways to see changing guards than just crowding against the fence at Buckingham Palace. First, visiting families should know that there are two separate guard ceremonies: the palace guard at Buckingham, and the mounted guard down the Mall at Whitehall.

Of the two, the mounted horse guards ceremony is more accessible. The site of the ceremony, a large open plaza called Horse Guards Parade, provides room to spread out and get a good view of the event. The Palace of Whitehall once stood in this part of London, and Horse Guards Parade was the tiltyard where jousting (tilting) tournaments were held. In a more modern incarnation, Horse Guards Parade was the site of the beach volleyball competition for the 2012 Olympics.

The guards are mounted troopers of the Household Cavalry, also known as the Sovereign's Life Guard. Hearing this name, children may ask, "If these guys are lifeguards, then where's the swimming pool?" There is no swimming pool, but if your kids love horses, this is the guard ceremony to see. The mounted horse guards are resplendent with their swords, shining silver breastplate armor, and beautifully groomed horses. Afterward, your children can pet the two horses standing guard on nearby on Whitehall Street. This makes an excellent photo op, but watch where you step!

The horse guards ceremony is a popular event that lasts about thirty minutes. Visitors can also glimpse the horse guards trooping to and from the ceremony. The guards form up at Wellington Barracks in Hyde Park at about 10:30 in the morning and return around noon.

In mid-June, Horse Guards Parade is the site of the ceremonial Trooping the Colour—a review of troops to mark the monarch's official birthday. Obtaining tickets to this popular event takes a lot of preplanning and some luck. It's somewhat easier to attend one of the rehearsals held on the weekends preceding the actual event. Also in June, military bands gather at Horse Guards Parade for the Beating Retreat ceremony. This is a chance to see marching bands and hear the tortured sounds of bagpipes in London.

If you are attending the Buckingham Palace guard ceremony, be sure to arrive early enough to get a spot up front against the palace

fence, so children have a good view. Even then, be prepared for pushing and jostling for position by other tourists. If it is too crowded for kids to see, climb up the steps of the nearby Queen Victoria Memorial for a better view. The ceremony is normally performed by the foot guards of the British Army's Household Division. In summer months, the guards wear bright red uniforms with tall bearskin hats. Uniforms vary depending on the season. The changing of the palace guard usually takes place daily at 11:00 a.m. during the summer and a fewer number of days during the rest of the year. Before the ceremony, a military band often plays in the palace courtyard. See if your kids can pick out what the band is playing. Their repertoire is not all old military marches. You are likely to hear more current popular music, but nothing too avant-garde (pardon the pun).

The changing of the Palace and Horse Guards is a complex military ballet crisscrossing the St. James's Park area from about 10:25 until 11:45 a.m. You can actually see more, and avoid the crush of the Buckingham Palace ceremony, by watching the guards form up and disband outside of Wellington Barracks and St. James's Palace. These are not as elaborate as the ceremony at Buckingham Palace, but they tend to be less crowded and onlookers are closer to the action.

Note that all times are subject to change.

Website: www.royal.gov.uk (search for "royal events and ceremonies")

Go for the Gold at Olympic Park

London is no newcomer to the Olympics. In 1908, the Summer Games were scheduled to be held in Rome, but plans were scuttled by the eruption of nearby Mt. Vesuvius. London stepped up to host what some call the first modern Olympics. In the aftermath of World War II, London helped restart the Olympics. Despite devastation and postwar shortages, London managed to stage the 1948 Olympics using Wembley Stadium for many events, and housing athletes at schools and former military camps all over the city.

Much changed in the sixty-four years between the 1948 London Olympics and the 2012 Summer Games. A dramatic change to

the London landscape was seen in a once-decrepit section of East London. The construction of Olympic Park transformed a wasteland into a modern sports complex. At just under one square mile, Queen Elizabeth Olympic Park is compact. It includes housing, shopping, parks, hotels, and offices—all served by a twenty-first-century public transportation network.

Calling the London Olympics site a former wasteland is no overstatement. The area was piled high with rubble dumped after World War II bombing attacks. There was so much debris that the River Lea, which runs through the area, was almost invisible. The soil was saturated with heavy metals and nasty industrial pollutants. This was about as far as you could get from the London that tourists want to enjoy.

The debris is long gone, the soil scrubbed clean, and a massive construction project transformed the area into an Olympics showcase. The River Lea was restored and thousands of trees were planted along its banks.

The future of Olympic Park is still being written. It was designed to have a life after the Olympic Games. Some of the big venues remain, some have been reconfigured, and some are gone. Professional football (soccer) matches are held in the Olympic Stadium. Swimming events continue at the aquatics center. What bigger thrill for the aspiring

young swimmers in your family than to plunge into the same pool where Michael Phelps won six medals. The London Aquatics Centre welcomes visitors, and a day pass is reasonably priced. Cyclists can take to the Olympic trail at the Lee Valley Velopark. The cycling center offers fully equipped mountain biking sessions for competent riders age ten and up and BMX sessions for riders age seven and up. Kids over age twelve can race around the iconic Olympic Velodrome track.

The less athletically inclined might opt for a ride to the top of the spiraling ArcelorMittal Orbit. The views are terrific and there's a fast way to get down too—the world's longest tunnel slide. In forty screaming seconds, adventurous visitors can zip around and down 580 feet from the top of the Orbit to ground level.

The park has some cool playgrounds. In the north end, kids can explore rock pools and tree houses, wander across wobbly bridges, and slide and swing in the Tumbling Bay playground. In the south, there are more play areas where children can climb rocks up to huge slides, enjoy oversized swings and get dirty in a giant sand pit. There is also a popular climbing wall and a computer-controlled fountain.

Sporting events will continue to draw visitors, and the former Olympics site has been transformed into a rather nice park. The adjoining Stratford City megamall is a retail destination. But whether the site ever qualifies as a top-tier London tourist destination remains to be seen.

Websites: www.arcelormittalorbit.com (observation tower)
www.queenelizabetholympicpark.co.uk (park)

Go Down the River

The Thames will take us to London town,
"Of wonderful beauty and great renown."
The dew goes up and the rain comes down,
To carry us safely to London town.
—"The Thames" by M. M. Hutchinson

A Mean Time in Greenwich

Here's a geography quiz for older kids: What is the latitude and longitude of London? Give up? At about fifty-two degrees north latitude, London is roughly in line with Calgary, Canada—a lot farther north than you might expect. The second part of the answer is more significant. London's longitude is nearly zero degrees. The city sits a few miles west of the prime meridian, the longitudinal line dividing the Earth into Eastern and Western Hemispheres. The suburban London town of Greenwich is home to the prime meridian.

Greenwich Mean Time is a standard used by scientists, navigators, militaries, and travelers throughout the world. Once they grasp the significance of Greenwich Mean Time, school-age kids can determine the time difference to their hometowns. Because time is such an important player here, it is hard to visit Greenwich and not check the time every minute or so.

Taking the boat down the Thames to Greenwich is fun even if your children don't care about longitude and Greenwich Mean Time. Most kids will enjoy a visit to the Royal Observatory in Greenwich, and they might learn something too. Interactive exhibits teach the importance of longitude in seaborne navigation. Early explorers often sailed in circles because they could measure latitude (distance from the equator) using the angle of the sun on the horizon, but they had no way to accurately measure longitude (distance east or west).

The Royal Observatory was founded in 1675 by King Charles II, who appointed John Flamsteed as the royal astronomer. John Flamsteed's marching orders were specific: find a way to measure longitude at sea. Given the competition among England, France, and Spain for control

of the world's oceans, solving the navigation problem was the Apollo moon project of its day. Mission Control—Greenwich's observatory building—was designed by Sir Christopher Wren.

A detailed explanation of longitudinal navigation is beyond the scope of this book, but the basic premise is that accurate timekeeping is essential to accurate navigation. Thus, timekeeping became a key function of the observatory. Every day at precisely 1:00 p.m., a red ball slides down a pole on top of the observatory. In times past, ships on the Thames would set their clocks ("chronometers" to you navigators) by this ball. As with many events in England, there is no reason to continue the tradition, but the time ball still drops each day, and tourists enjoy it. Greenwich Mean Time remains a world standard for timekeeping, although technically Coordinated Universal Time has replaced it.

Continuing with Longitudinal Navigation 101: another key to navigation is establishing a uniform starting point—the zero or

prime meridian line. In 1884, the International Meridian Conference set that line in Greenwich and established the concept of twenty-four worldwide time zones. The prime meridian runs right through the Royal Observatory and is marked on the pavement and walls of the building. A green laser light cuts across the nighttime Greenwich skies highlighting the meridian. At the observatory, this dividing line provides entertainment for visitors, who can stand with one foot in the Western Hemisphere and one foot in the Eastern (or put a foot on the line and balance between east and west).

You can explore Greenwich's association with the sea at other local sites including the Old Royal Naval College and the National Maritime Museum. The Maritime Museum is a mixture of high tech and history. There are plenty of pictures of old dead navy guys and fleets of model ships, as well as interesting audiovisual and computer simulations.

The nautical museum's Exploration Wing galleries include Pacific Exploration, Polar Worlds, Tudor and Stuart Seafarers, and Sea Things. While most of those names are pretty self-explanatory, Sea Things is dedicated to nautical curiosities. Younger children will enjoy the Ahoy! play area. Older kids can explore the museum's Seahorse ship mock-up and fight pirates through interactive games.

The Maritime Museum also houses the Nelson, Navy, Nation Gallery. Or perhaps we should call it the Admiral Nelson shrine. The gallery is dominated by Nelson memorabilia, including the bullet-holed dress uniform worn when Nelson was killed at the Battle of Trafalgar. There is plenty of dry historical material here—items that many kids will skip—but some of the computer-animated displays will attract young sailors.

While in Greenwich you can tour one of the world's most famous sailing ships. The permanently dry-docked Cutty Sark is the last of the clipper ships that sailed around Cape Horn bringing tea from China. The ship survived thousands of nautical miles but nearly perished in a dramatic 2007 fire. It has been beautifully restored.

Greenwich Market, just a few steps from the Cutty Sark, is a good spot to grab a bite to eat and browse the stalls. The market features antiques and collectibles on Tuesday, Thursday, and Friday. Crafts and food dominate other days.

Another Greenwich gem is the Queen's House. Take a close look at

this small palace. It seems awfully familiar, doesn't it? When American visitors learn that this building was once known as the White House, the connection becomes uncanny. The name refers to the building's white plaster facade, but the architecture could have been a model for the White House in Washington. Amazingly, in compact Greenwich, three landmarks have been designated as World Heritage Sites by the United Nations: the Queen's House, the former Royal Naval College, and the Old Royal Observatory.

There is a restaurant, café, and snack bar in the Nautical Museum. The observatory and the Cutty Sark each have a café. There are toilets and baby changing areas in several locations. Most areas of Greenwich museums are wheelchair accessible, but parts of the observatory and the Cutty Sark have limited access.For more information, see the Royal Museums Greenwich website at www.rmg.co.uk

Greenwich is also a stop on the Sir Walter Raleigh trivia tour. A muddy Greenwich street is supposedly where Sir Walter laid his cloak over a puddle to protect the feet of Queen Elizabeth I. The royal family hardly returned the favor. Raleigh was later imprisoned in the Tower of London and eventually executed.

Given Greenwich's association with timekeeping and navigation, it became a focal point for the year 2000 millennium celebrations. A theme park called the Millennium Dome, now known as the O2 Arena, was built nearby. Once featured in a James Bond movie, the structure was planned as a one-year exhibition during 2000, but the venue continues to be used for concerts and events. The O2 Arena is located along the Thames, just downriver from old Greenwich. At more than 1,000 feet in diameter and 160 feet high, the dome is undeniably huge. Adventure seekers can even buy a ticket and clamber across the sloping roof. For details see the O2 website at www.theo2.co.uk

Just five miles down the Thames from central London, Greenwich is easy to reach by boat, the Tube, or the Docklands Light Railway. As you might expect, most children vote for the boat trip. Here is a rundown of the easiest ways to get to Greenwich:

- Taking the Tube? The Underground's Jubilee Line goes to the Greenwich North station, the closest stop for the O2, but not very close to other Greenwich sites.

- Want to try the Docklands Light Railway? This automated above ground commuter line has a station just steps from the Cutty Sark in Greenwich. The Docklands Light Railway connects with the Tube near the Tower of London.

- Thinking about a boat? If you have time and the weather is good, a boat cruise is a perfect way to see the Thames and get to Greenwich.

- What about a cable car? That's right, modern cable cars whisk visitors over the Thames near the O2. The views are worth a round-trip.
- It is also possible to reach Greenwich by train from several London rail stations. The Greenwich rail station is about a ten-minute walk to the town's tourist attractions. The Maze Hill station is a five-minute walk to the National Maritime Museum. There are also local buses from Greenwich rail station.

Thames River Barrier

Visitors to Greenwich can continue down the Thames to visit a modern engineering wonder—the flood barriers that protect London from the ravages of the rising river. If your kids are fascinated by dams, bridges, and other big public works projects, they may enjoy a visit to the Thames River Barrier Information Centre. Once the most futuristic structure on the Thames, the barrier is now a minor tourist attraction. However, residents upstream in Greenwich would never take the barrier for granted. Without it, parts of their town would be under water during tidal surges.

This is one of the world's largest movable flood barriers. When it is raised, its clamshell floodgates are each five stories high. If you arrive on the day of the scheduled monthly test, you don't have to wait for a flood to see the barriers in action. But even when the barriers are not operating, the visitor center offers informative exhibits and working models. A park with a play area and restaurant overlooks the barrier on the north side of the river, but there is no direct access between the park and the information center. There are also river sightseeing cruises that sail past the Thames Barrier but do not stop.

Website: www.gov.uk/the-thames-barrier

Go Up the River

Some of the world's best gardens are at Kew, just a few miles upstream from central London. A trip up the River Thames also leads to one of Britain's most historic palaces, Henry VIII's Hampton Court.

Kew—The Smell of Flowers

> Mistress Mary, quite contrary,
>
> How does your garden grow?
>
> With silver bells, and cockle shells,
>
> And marigolds all in a row.
>
> —Traditional children's rhyme

Parks have gardens, palaces have gardens, churches have gardens... visitors are never far from a garden in London. It is easy to get garden overload during a visit. But if you want to see the mother of all gardens, then add one more stop: the Royal Botanic Gardens, better known as Kew Gardens.

Kew Gardens has a more important mission than simply providing a lovely spot for visitors to enjoy. Plant conservation is the real goal here and Kew's collection contains living specimens of more than ten percent of the world's flowering plants. Another important task at Kew Gardens is to preserve seed samples from all the plants on Earth.

For the casual visitor, the real attractions at Kew are the acres of landscaped gardens and glasshouses full of unusual plant displays. There is enough variety to keep green-thumbed visitors fascinated for days. The rest of us, especially those with children, will want to devote two or three hours to simply walking the grounds.

Kew's elaborate glasshouses are full of surprises. The world's oldest potted plant is at Kew, and anyone who has killed a houseplant will be amazed that this plant has survived since 1775. Kew also claims the world's tallest indoor plant, a replacement for the previous

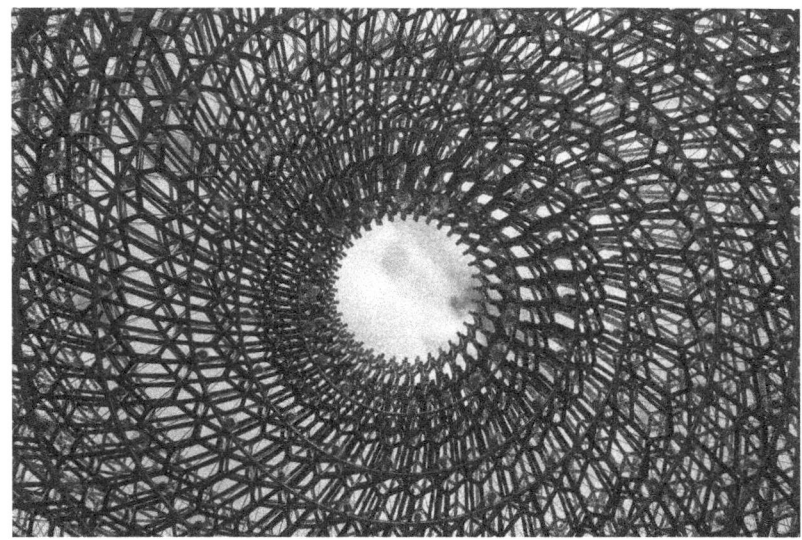

record-holding palm, which literally hit the roof in 2001 and had to be cut down. Children may or may not be impressed with all the plants, but they likely will want to climb the spiral staircase up to the elevated walkway that encircles the top of the Palm House. If you lose track of your child here, look up.

Elsewhere in Kew, visitors can take a stroll in the treetops via the outdoor Treetop Walkway. Designed by the architects of the London Eye, the walkway is nearly 60 feet high and spans more than 600 feet, allowing visitors to experience life in the trees of Kew Gardens.

Kew's Climbers and Creepers exhibit is a plant-themed indoor/outdoor playground that mixes learning with play. Kids ages three to nine are free to crawl on and through giant "plants" here. Treehouse Towers, Kew's outdoor playground, is a wonderful play option in nice weather for children ages three to eleven.

But the Kew wonder that has many visitors buzzing is The Hive. Looking very much like a modern art interpretation of a beehive, the fifty-five foot Hive is alive with sound. Bees communicate through vibrations and this exhibit is actually plugged into a real beehive on the grounds of Kew Gardens. Vibration is synthesized into sound, music, and light. Walking through The Hive is a multi-sensory experience—you will feel connected to the live bees of Kew's bee colony.

Although they are nearly eclipsed by the grandeur of the gardens, a small palace and a quaint royal getaway are also tucked into Kew Gardens. Built in 1631, Kew Palace is the smallest royal palace in England. It was home to King George III, who spent time here while suffering from his madness. In 1761, he gave Queen Charlotte a nice little wedding present: a rustic cottage on the Kew grounds equipped with a menagerie of kangaroos, buffalo, and other exotic animals. The cottage and surrounding property remained in the royal family until Queen Victoria turned them over to Kew Gardens in 1897.

There are restaurants on the premises, but Kew is a wonderful place to picnic. Its wide-open grounds and fragrant displays are a relaxing contrast to the bustle of urban sites in downtown London.

Websites: www.kew.org (Kew Gardens)
www.hrp.org.uk (Kew Palace)

Kew—The Hiss of Steam

If you have made the trek to Kew and are not completely exhausted from roaming the gardens, consider visiting some sights nearby. The London Museum of Water and Steam is across Kew Bridge from the Royal Botanic Gardens. The museum features several working steam pump engines, an electricity exhibit, a small steam railway, and an outdoor Splash Zone play area. Kew's steam engines once pumped the water supply for West London, and although the waterworks have been modernized, the giant pumping engines are still on display. On

weekends, the museum powers up its huge Cornish steam engines, which is great for kids who like the noise and power of big machines.

There is a café and picnic area onsite. Toilets are available. Most areas of the museum are wheelchair accessible.

Website: www.waterandsteam.org.uk

Kew—The Sound of Music

The Musical Museum at Kew Bridge falls into a quirky category of tourist venues. It will never appear on a list of top London area attractions. But if you are in the vicinity and have an appreciation for automatic musical instruments, plan a brief visit. You will be treated to lots of music, but remarkably few musicians. Here the instruments play themselves: organs, music boxes, pianos, violins, and the Clarabella—sort of a one-man band without the man.

The museum has limited opening hours, but often features special programs and performances. There is a tearoom onsite. Toilets are available and the museum is wheelchair accessible.

Website: www.musicalmuseum.co.uk

Hampton Court Palace—*Oh, Henry!*

My, you ought to seen old Henry the Eight when he was in bloom. He was a blossom. He used to marry a new wife every day, and chop off her head next morning...

—*The Adventures of Huckleberry Finn* by Mark Twain

Much of the intrigue of Henry VIII's reign took place at Hampton Court. Some of Henry's wives enjoyed living at the palace—briefly—before adjourning to accommodations in the Tower of London—again, briefly, and in most cases terminally.

Uber-ambitious cardinal Thomas Wolsey built Hampton Court Palace in the early 1500s. King Henry VIII decided that he liked the palace so much that he wanted one just like it. But instead of building his own, Henry VIII simply confiscated Hampton Court Palace from Wolsey. Henry then expanded Cardinal Wolsey's residence, and Henry's successors altered the building even more, but portions of the original brick Tudor palace are still visible today. The building changed significantly in the 1600s under King William III, who planned to turn the site into an English version of Versailles. William employed Christopher Wren, architect of St. Paul's Cathedral, to convert Hampton Court into one of the finest palaces in Britain.

How to convince your children to visit yet another palace? Not to worry. In addition to history and architectural splendor, Hampton Court features Henry VIII's original indoor tennis court, a fantastic garden maze, one of the world's largest grapevines, carriage rides on the grounds, a super fun play area, and lots of outdoor space to explore.

When we think about Henry VIII, we often see a picture of Henry the Huge. But in his earlier years, the king was fairly athletic and a great tennis fan. In 1530, he had a tennis court built at Hampton Court Palace. Royal tennis is only vaguely like the modern version because this indoor game was played off the walls and ledges surrounding the court. Legend has it that Henry played tennis here while Anne Boleyn was being executed at the Tower of London. The royal tennis court is open to Hampton Court Palace visitors. King Charles II renovated the court in the late 1600s, and what visitors see today has been essentially unchanged since 1700, the obvious exception being the modern lighting. The court is still in use by members of the local tennis club and you may be lucky enough to see a game in progress. If so, please observe one basic rule of royal tennis etiquette: spectators must keep quiet!

One of the most popular features of Hampton Court is the maze built on the palace grounds for King William III. Some kids attack the problem of the maze logically, tracking their position by the angle of the sun, or taking only left turns, or using some other semi-scientific approach. Others abandon all logic and just run helter-skelter through the maze. We don't know which way works best, but the maze is a fun-filled challenge for adults and children alike.

During summer months, Hampton Court opens the gates to the Magic Garden—a massive playground guarded by a rather large dragon. Kids love to climb and scamper across the playground to discover the garden's mythical beasts. They can storm the battlements and besiege the towers to their hearts' content. This is a popular venue and  one that parents may have a hard time getting children to leave. So plan accordingly.

Another interesting stop on the palace grounds is the Great Vine of 1769. The vine is one of the world's largest single grapevines, so immense that it has its own greenhouse and root care field. The old vine is still going, producing a large crop of grapes every year. The palace gardens alone are worth the trip to Hampton Court. Entry to the palace's formal gardens is included with overall admission, or you can purchase garden-only tickets. But it costs nothing to visit much of the grounds, so many tourists and local residents simply stroll around or picnic near the palace.

Although many of Hampton Court's highlights are on the outside, the palace interior is stellar in its own right. Part Versailles, part Tudor brick palace, it is unlike any other palace in Europe. Children are often interested in the cavernous Tudor kitchens, which look as if cooks are in the midst of preparing a feast, or maybe just a snack to satisfy Henry VIII's appetite. Adults gaze slack-jawed at Henry VIII's opulent

Chapel Royal and William III's baroque state apartments.

Hampton Court is also the site of a mammoth flower show held each July. Visitors who arrive during the show can expect large crowds, but they will be able to tour a phenomenal gardening exhibition. Admission to the show is separate from admission to the palace, and the show tickets are fairly expensive for the casual visitor.

In December and January, a temporary ice-skating rink is set up in front of the palace, livening up the site during an otherwise slow tourism period. There are other special events scattered throughout the regular season.

Hampton Court has a restaurant and cafés. A large tearoom is located on the old palace tiltyard, so you can enjoy your tea where Tudor knights once jousted. There are plenty of picnic spots, toilets, and baby changing areas at Hampton Court. Some rooms of the palace are not wheelchair accessible.

Website: www.hrp.org.uk

Field Trips
from London

London Is Great. Why Leave?

London has enough to keep a touring family busy for weeks, so why even consider traveling outside this fascinating city? Well, for overseas visitors, it seems a shame to travel all the way to Britain and not see more of the country than just the capital. The remedy is a field trip. Rent a car or take a train and explore some piece of England. This is a compact and eminently accessible land.

The focus of this book is London, and close by places such as Greenwich and Hampton Court. But we will also give you a taste of what lies farther afield by describing a few gems in the surrounding areas:

- Nearby Windsor with its famous castle
- Oxford's Blenheim Palace
- The Rollright Stones

In addition, we will provide some survival tips in case you consider driving in Britain.

Off to Windsor

Although Windsor is within London's suburbs, a family trip here is the perfect opportunity to get away from downtown, see a little of the countryside, and visit a historic town on the Thames. Windsor Castle, the central focus of the town, is one of the most elaborate castles or palaces in the greater London area. Windsor is an easy thirty- to fifty-minute train ride from downtown London, so this first field trip requires no driving.

The Castle

More than 900 years ago, William the Conqueror chose the site for Windsor Castle on a hill above the River Thames. Like the Tower of London, Windsor was part of the Norman king's plans to subdue and maintain control over England. The strategically placed castle was one day's march from London and it guarded the city's western flank. Subsequent kings and queens used Windsor as a part-time residence and a refuge from wars, plagues, and uprisings. What has evolved at Windsor is part Norman castle and part royal palace.

Unlike Hampton Court Palace, Windsor Castle is still used by Britain's royal family. Because the castle is a home, during your visit you may observe pet cats, resident children walking to school, or staff members off to play tennis. Just like at Buckingham Palace, keep an eye on the flagpole. A Union Jack means nothing special. But if the royal standard (the lion flag) appears above Windsor's Norman keep, you will know that the royals have arrived. During one of our visits, the Union Jack was flying when we entered the castle. After our tour, we stopped in the toilets. When we came out, the royal standard was flying. We missed the arrival of the queen while we were in the loo!

The whole family will enjoy a visit to Windsor Castle. Some rooms have extensive displays of armor, which many kids find interesting, but all those staid, ornate royal apartments can get tedious. So a

Windsor highlight for many children is Queen Mary's dollhouse. This is one of the largest, most elaborate dollhouses imaginable, truly fit for a queen. The castle also offers family activity trail guides.

During a few weeks each year, usually in August and September, visitors can climb to the top of Windsor's Round Tower. A separate behind-the-scenes tour of the castle's Great Kitchen is also available.

For kids who have not had their fill of changing guards, Windsor Castle boasts a fairly impressive ceremony, usually held on several days each week at 11:00 am. Check the Windsor Castle section on the Royal Collection website for details.

One of the most impressive buildings in the castle complex is St. George's Chapel, completed in 1475 and a stellar example of medieval architecture. Eighteen kings and queens are buried here, so yes, Windsor has a full complement of "old dead guys." The chapel is often staffed with enthusiastic, knowledgeable volunteer tour guides. On one visit, a grandfatherly volunteer took extra time to show off the chapel to our kids, pointing out items of interest to children. It was a welcome personal touch. The chapel is closed to the public on Sunday and frequently for special events.

Touring Windsor Castle today, visitors see no real evidence of the major fire that destroyed parts of the castle in 1992, but the fire is still a relatively fresh memory here. Young visitors might be interested in the story of the fire and the heroic efforts to save priceless art and furnishings from the burning building. About one-fifth of the castle was damaged or destroyed. Restoration was completed in 1997 at the cost of almost £36.5 million. Ironically, the loss at Windsor was actually a gain for London tourists, since Buckingham Palace was first opened to visitors in part to help raise money to restore Windsor Castle.

Windsor is a pleasant place to take a walk. The Long Walk is an arrow-straight road that runs from Windsor Castle to a statue of King George III nearly three miles away. Closed to most traffic, the roadway is lined by the trees and fields of Windsor Home Park. This is an ideal spot to let children burn off excess energy. They can take off running down the Long Walk, but of course you may have to chase them.

Occasionally, visitors to Windsor Home Park can also tour Frogmore House, a royal country estate and the burial place of Queen Victoria and Prince Albert. This was a royal house, not a palace, and

it is a contrast to formal Windsor Castle. The house and gardens are usually open two weekends a year, once in May and again in late August. Group tours are possible at other times.

The Windsor Castle complex has a family restroom and baby changing room. Most areas are wheelchair accessible. Be sure to check the website for opening times.

Website: www.royalcollection.org.uk (select the "Windsor" section)

Windsor—In and Around Town

The town of Windsor is an amalgamation of peaceful life along the Thames, English history, and some tacky tourist-oriented businesses. It is disconcerting to see a McDonald's or a Starbucks just outside the massive ancient walls of Windsor Castle. But Windsor's many restaurants, souvenir shops, and tourist traps are fairly concentrated and the rest of the town is generally unaffected.

While you are in Windsor, take the pedestrian bridge across the Thames to the tiny town of Eton, which offers some antique shops, a few pubs, and a glimpse of the famous boys' school whose students have included royal princes. Touring Eton College is a bit like visiting Harry Potter's Hogwarts Academy. No magic classes and Quidditch matches here, but the buildings and atmosphere of this ancient school seem vaguely familiar to Potter fans. For information about weekly summer tours, check the school's website at www.etoncollege.com

More than anything else, Eton is a quiet town on the river, a contrast to tourist-thronged Windsor. And the farther you walk into Eton and away from Windsor, the less touristy the town becomes. In Eton, pubs are more likely to be filled with locals and shops are less likely to hawk cheap souvenirs.

All the King's Swans

Walking over the Windsor-Eton pedestrian bridge, you might catch sight of dozens of swans swimming against the strong current or coasting downstream. On one visit our children counted sixty birds

near the bridge.

Since the twelfth century, all the swans on the Thames have been owned by the royal family or by two other groups: the Vintners and the Dyers. In a land of quaint tradition, it is not surprising that a special swan-upping (tagging) ceremony is held on the Thames in July. There is even an official Royal Master of the Swans who supervises the tagging of swans and cygnets. The swan-upping on the Thames has become something of a tourist attraction, although the typical tourist may have trouble attending because the event moves along the river between the towns of Walton-on-Thames and Whitchurch.

The swans at Windsor are so-called mute swans, but they are anything but mute, hissing and honking endlessly. The historical fuss over swan ownership was based on the fact that swans were once an important royal food group. If this situation had continued to the present day, the Windsor McDonald's might be serving McSwan sandwiches. Fortunately, swans are not on the menu, but they do add to the atmosphere along the Thames at Windsor.

Lego Invades Windsor

Families visiting Windsor may find it hard to ignore the fact that Legoland is only three miles down the road from Windsor Castle. The intrusion of modern life on historic Windsor is epitomized by the Lego theme park.

Visitors can go from the 900-year-old stones of Windsor Castle to the new plastic bricks of Legoland Windsor in about ten minutes via a shuttle bus from both Windsor rail stations. The question is, do you want to? For children under age twelve who love to play with Legos, this theme park will probably be a big hit. Older children may be disappointed because much of the park is geared to younger kids. But Lego bricks have been around since 1958, and we suspect that even many older "children" will want to visit Legoland.

The park's rides are pretty tame by modern theme park standards. One ride for the younger set gives kids the chance to practice driving through an elaborate mock-up of city streets. Chaos and fun ensue, especially for non-British children who have to adjust to British traffic rules.

But the real jaw dropping sights for the true Lego fans are in Miniland, with its detailed cities and landscapes built entirely from the plastic blocks. The model of London is phenomenal, although the cynic may point out the irony of paying to see a Lego model of London when the real thing is just a few miles away.

Legoland is a clean, well-run park designed to market the Lego brand, but don't expect many free product giveaways or bargain-priced Legos for sale. Although the gift shops overflow with Lego merchandise, the prices are basically retail.

True Lego fans can spend the night in the Legoland Castle Hotel, where the Lego theme carries over into Pirate, Kingdom, and Adventure family bedrooms.

There are restaurants and snack bars onsite as well as outdoor picnic spots. No shortage of toilets and baby changing areas and there are storage lockers and strollers/pushchairs available for rent. Most areas of the park are wheelchair accessible, although some rides have restrictions. Opening hours and admission prices vary by season.

Website: www.legoland.co.uk

Off to Oxfordshire

Visitors to Windsor never really leave suburban London, but those who venture farther northwest to Oxfordshire can truly escape the city. Tourist agencies differ on where the heart of England lies. But if this is not quite England's heart, with Oxford University at its center, Oxfordshire may qualify as England's brain.

There are many reasons to visit. The city of Oxford and its university are obvious destinations. Oxfordshire is also known as a gateway to the undeniably quaint Cotswolds region, and Stratford-upon-Avon is just a few miles northwest. But because our goal is to give just a taste of the region, we will do that by describing two local attractions: the grandeur of Blenheim Palace, and the mystery of the Rollright Stones.

Blenheim Palace

The year is 1704. What can a nobleman do to earn the absolute gratitude of England's Queen Anne? Why, defeat the French, of course. That is exactly what John Churchill did, and Blenheim Palace was his reward. Churchill, the first Duke of Marlborough, received the Royal Manor of Woodstock and the queen's promise to pay for the construction of Blenheim Palace. After falling out of royal favor, Churchill completed the palace at his own expense. In the years that followed, his descendants surrounded Blenheim with some of the country's most fantastic gardens.

If you spend much time traveling around Britain, grand palaces and stellar gardens become almost commonplace. But even to a veteran tourist, Blenheim Palace is something special. Gazing at the exterior of the palace, you may catch yourself humming the theme music from *Downton Abbey*. This is a palace of royal proportions, but it is also a private home. Inside, the grandeur continues. The Long Library is one of the longest rooms in any private home in England. The library at Blenheim Palace contains thousands of books and one heck of a sound system—a cathedral-sized pipe organ at the end of the vast room.

The Churchill name brings many visitors to Blenheim. The palace tour includes the room where Winston Churchill was born in 1874, and Churchill memorabilia and photographs are on display. This is an ideal location to explain to children the importance of Winston Churchill, perhaps linking the man to sites they have visited in London, such as the Churchill War Rooms. Kids may be interested to learn that Churchill's mother was an American, and that Winston Churchill was one of only a handful of people to be granted honorary US citizenship. Churchill is buried in the nearby Oxfordshire town of Bladon.

The 2,100 acres of gardens and park around the palace are as impressive as the building itself. The gardens were designed by Lancelot "Capability" Brown, the architect of England's finest gardens. Blenheim Lake and the surrounding gardens are among Brown's top examples of landscape magic. Families can rent rowboats here or take a motor launch trip on the lake.

Blenheim is no mere relic. The palace is home to the current

Duke of Marlborough and his family. Upkeep on the palace and the park is not cheap, so the duke opened much of Blenheim to tourists and added some attractions to entice visitors. The latter may seem

unnecessary to adults who are interested in seeing the landscape artistry of Capability Brown or visiting the birthplace of Winston Churchill. But for kids, the duke's amusement park additions are great fun. So while you are touring the palace, promise your children a ride on the miniature train. While you are ogling the rose gardens, remind the kids that they will get to run through the palace's maze. Younger children can romp in the adventure play area. And everyone will love the Blenheim Butterfly House where exotic butterflies flutter.

The Blenheim Palace calendar is loaded with special events: open air cinema, a car rally, proms (music), picnic concerts and more. See the Blenheim website for details.

How to get there? Driving is most direct, but there is train service from London to Oxford, with a connecting bus to Blenheim Palace.

There are restaurants, cafés, and picnic areas onsite. Toilets and baby changing areas are available. Some parts of the palace and grounds are not wheelchair accessible.

Website: www.blenheimpalace.com

In Search of Stones

Nearly everyone has heard of Stonehenge, but many tourists may be surprised to learn that Britain is dotted with many other stone circles. Some circles are large and well known, but others are obscure structures lying in the middle of cow pastures. Although the major sites have been excavated, x-rayed, and studied by scholars, the smaller stone circles are explained best by local legends.

The Rollright Stones are located in pastureland near the tiny village of Long Compton, not far from the Oxfordshire town of Chipping Norton. On one trip, after severely taxing our navigation skills, we managed to find this stone circle.

The gatekeeper, in a tiny shack, charged our two children fifty pence admission each. But he promised that they could get the money back if they correctly counted the number of stones in the circle.

The stone circle contains some very eroded stones and some that are nearly buried in the ground, and the actual number of stones was

the subject of debate. The children each reported different numbers to the gatekeeper, who informed them they were both wrong, but he still cheerfully refunded their fifty pence.

In the Oxfordshire fields, we heard several legends associated with the Rollright Stones. The best-known story is documented to at least the 1500s, so it is not something the locals recently made up at the village pub. (More likely they made it up at the pub 500 years ago.)

A king and his men were traveling through the area on their way to conquer England. They were intercepted by a local witch, who made what seemed to be a great offer to the king:

> Seven long strides shalt thou take
> *And if Long Compton thou canst see,*
> *King of England thou shalt be.*

"Hot diggity," said the king as he strapped on his running shoes. No, that's wrong. What really happened was that the king strode confidently across the field shouting:

> *Stick, stock, stone.*
> *As King of England I shall be known.*

But the king did not count on the slight rise in the ground that blocked his view of Long Compton village. After the king took his seventh step, the witch laughed and crowed, "I'll get you my pretty, and your little dog too!" No, sorry for the confusion. These witch stories all sound alike. What she really said was:

> *As Long Compton thou canst not see*
> *King of England thou shalt not be.*
> *Rise up stick and stand still stone*
> *For King of England thou shalt be none;*
> *Thou and thy men hoar stones shall be*
> *And I myself an elder tree.*

This was the witch's way of transforming the king into the King Stone that stands across the road from the Rollright Stones and the king's men into the nearby Kings Men Stone Circle. And with the last line of the spell, the witch went into retirement as an elder tree.

There are no facilities at the Rollright Stones and the site is not wheelchair accessible. For information, see the Rollright Stones website at www.rollrightstones.co.uk or the English Heritage website at www.english-heritage.org.uk/rollrightstones

If you visit a stone circle during the summer solstice—the longest day of the year—you may be confronted with a different kind of tourist. The first clue might be the large number of vintage minivans parked nearby or impromptu campsites scattered in surrounding fields. On one of our visits around the time of the summer solstice, we noticed a long line of No Parking signs and traffic cones on the road at an isolated stone circle. Two National Trust vans were parked nearby, and several uniformed men were milling about. We stopped to talk with them. Careful not to offend, the National Trust rangers admitted that they were present to guard against an influx of solstice celebrators. The previous year, scads of people had overrun the site and caused damage. The problem became so acute at Stonehenge that local authorities once closed off the site entirely on the summer solstice. Now they admit limited numbers of solstice celebrators.

Baby, You Can Drive My Car

There is plenty of bucolic British countryside within a relatively short drive from London. Although the prospect of driving on the left can be daunting for some visitors, it is well worth the effort.

Country Churches

When driving the back roads of rural Britain, allow time to stop and visit village churches, not necessarily as a religious experience but for the history and local atmosphere. Churches were once the focal point of village life in Britain and they all have a story to tell, usually explained in a fifty-pence brochure sold inside the church.

Gustav Holtz was the organist at the church in the tiny Cotswolds village of Wyck Rissington. He went on to fame as the composer of musical works such as The Planets. This historical side note was less fascinating to our children than the story of an elaborate maze formerly located near the village church. Fearing that too many visitors would overrun the site, its builder razed the maze. There is only a commemorative mosaic plaque remaining on the church wall.

Church graveyards provide a resting place for the dead, but they can also serve as a temporary resting spot for the weary tourist. Ancient cemeteries are a good place to sit and absorb some of the quiet village atmosphere. The dead don't mind if you discreetly munch a picnic snack while sitting on a cemetery bench, reading stone inscriptions and contemplating their lives.

You will find another type of religious site in British towns and countryside. Hundreds of abbeys and cathedrals stand in ruined glory, a legacy of religious strife in the nation's history. Try to visit at least one of these interesting ruins. Visit too many and kids may begin to complain, "Geez, *another* old wrecked church?"

Now that we have whetted your appetite for a field trip, it is time to review some practical matters about traveling around Britain.

Hit the Road

Unless you have the nerves of a big-city taxicab driver, don't even think of driving in central London. But if you are planning an extended trip outside the city, consider renting a vehicle and exploring Britain. North American visitors should keep in mind that cars (and many roads) are small by American standards. And fuel costs are high in Britain. Consider arranging the rental online before leaving home because local rentals are sometimes more expensive than those made in advance. Before paying for optional collision insurance, contact your credit card company to see if coverage is automatically included when you charge the rental. Travel insurance policies also often include rental car coverage.

"Drive a car on the wrong side of the road? You've got to be kidding!" That is a common reaction from non-British tourists. Generally, driving on the left is less of a challenge than you might imagine. It helps that the driver's seat is on the right, along with the appropriate controls. No, the gas and brake pedals are not reversed, but the gearshift is on the left, and that means shifting with your left hand, which may overtax your dexterity. We recommend renting a car with automatic transmission despite the extra cost.

Once on the road, repeat this mantra: keep left, keep LEFT, KEEP LEFT! Actually, this is not overly difficult, because everybody else is keeping left, too. Just follow them. Maybe the most challenging maneuver is turning right at an intersection and remembering to head for the left lane as you get on the next road.

Traffic circles (roundabouts) are common, and there is a learning curve for the driving tourist. Yield to the traffic in the circle—it will be coming from your right—but once you are in the circle, yield to no one. In a multi-lane roundabout, the outside lane is for immediate exits and the inner lanes are for those continuing around the circle. Move left to exit out of the circle and use your turn signal to indicate whether you are turning out or staying in the roundabout. Miss your turnoff? Just keep going around the circle. Explaining this is harder than driving it, assuming you KEEP LEFT!

Driving in unfamiliar territory on the "wrong" side of the road is a lot easier if one person navigates while the other drives. Make sure you have a GPS device, a mobile phone with a map app, and/or detailed printed maps. Carefully plan your routes in advance and keep your sense of humor when you get lost.

As in any country, if you drive the superhighways you will miss much of the countryside and small towns. Britain's M roads are similar to American interstate highways, French autoroutes, or German autobahns. The more interesting routes are usually smaller A- or B-class roads, but you need good maps to negotiate the back roads. Where there's a choice, take the road that goes through an ancient village or requires a short ferryboat ride. You will know that you are on the scenic route when the road is narrower than your driveway back home.

Time and Distance

Although England is a small country, we wonder sometimes if the English mile is the same unit of measurement as the North American mile. Miles don't mean much in cities, where distances are usually measured in blocks. But while driving in the English countryside, we once spotted a sign that read "Nottingham 9 miles." The town was not on our planned itinerary, but it seemed a reasonable detour because the children wanted to see Sherwood Forest. We got off the M superhighway and started along smaller roads toward Nottingham. We drove and drove, and drove some more before finally arriving in the legendary town about forty minutes later. We concluded that traveling those nine miles fully explains the origins of the phrase "around Robin Hood's barn."

Miles? Isn't the United Kingdom on the metric system? Well, yes and no. Road distances and speed limits are shown in miles, but just about everything else is metric.

Here is the important lesson we learned after driving thousands of miles on British roads. It is driving time, not distance, that matters most in planning a trip. Always allow extra driving time for contingencies:

- Narrow, winding roads—our favorites in Cornwall were about ten feet wide total, for both directions.
- Cattle and sheep crossings—livestock crossings marked by flashing warning lights.
- Roadwork—even on the smallest backcountry roads you will

find work being done, but no flagmen or flagwomen. Britons use automatic portable traffic signals to direct traffic at road construction sites.

- Gypsy caravans—real Gypsies, in colorful horse-drawn wagons, going three miles per hour in a no-passing zone. Gypsies are a rare sight in twenty-first-century Britain, but there are still a few travelers on the road. Consider yourself lucky if you see them, despite the traffic delay.
- Unmarked roads—tiny roads are usually signposted toward somewhere, but may not have a route number or name.
- Farm traffic—nothing compares with following a fertilizer wagon for a few fragrant, winding miles.

Train Wizardry

Arriving at King's Cross rail station, Britain's most famous modern-day wizard was as confused as any London tourist. To catch the Hogwarts Express train, Harry Potter searched the station for the elusive, invisible Platform Nine $^3/_4$. Although most of us Muggles won't face this problem, Harry's experience proves that it pays to know what you are doing before walking into a London rail station.

Using trains, you can add day trips to your visit. Your family can explore beyond London without renting a car. Wonderful spots like Windsor and Hampton Court are less than an hour by train from London. In two hours, you can journey to the fascinating cities of Bath, Oxford, or York.

Rail travel works well with restless children because they can move around, look out the windows, amuse other passengers, get a snack, and visit the loo . . . without stopping or slowing down progress toward your destination. Here are some train travel tips:

- Round-trip tickets are called return tickets in Britain. For day trips outside London, advance purchase and off-peak day return fares are often the best deals.

- Rail passes, such as the Britrail Pass. can be a good deal for those planning extensive rail travel in the United Kingdom. For a few day trips out of London, a rail pass is not always necessary or economical. Note that many discount railcards issued in the United Kingdom are for UK residents only.

- Standard-class seats are usually sufficient and first-class accommodations are not often worth the cost difference on short rail journeys.

- Do a little homework and try to sit on the side of the train with the best view. For example, if you are traveling on a coastal railway, sit on the side facing the water.

- Seat reservations are a good idea on busy trains, and they are required on some routes. Buy tickets and make reservations at major rail stations or online.

- Avoid the front rail cars ("coaches" or "carriages" in Britspeak). Air pressure changes when entering tunnels can cause ear discomfort, particularly for young children.

- Some train cars are set up with four facing seats and a table between. Reserve one of these so young kids can read, play games, or eat a snack and you can keep tabs on them. But don't sit here if no one wants to ride facing backward.

- Seat reservations may be displayed on screens above the seats. The conductor (ticket inspector) may also stick a ticket on top of the seatback to mark it as taken. Check that you are not sitting in someone else's seat.

- On some trains, you can sit in quiet coaches where mobile phones and audible music are banned. Children are allowed, but noisy kids may elicit scowls.

- Rail stations do not always have lifts (elevators). If family members can't carry luggage up and down stairs, then you face a challenge. Most stations have luggage carts but no porters, and carts are useless on stairways. Allow plenty of extra time to lug that luggage or risk missing a train.

- In London, the main rail stations are all on one level or they have lifts, so luggage toting is not a big problem. However, some London Underground/Tube stations do not have lifts or escalators.

- Some smaller stations are fully automated, with electronic ticket vending machines and computer screens that announce arrivals and departures. This may be disconcerting if you are looking for an information counter or ticket booth. With a little practice, and adequate time before your train departs, the automated system works well, although automated ticket machines may not always function for travelers without chip-and-pin credit cards.

- Train travel is a picnic opportunity. The food served on trains is mediocre, and it can be expensive.
- British railway employees sometimes go on strike and disrupt rail service. That is a problem for tourists on a schedule who can't just hop into the family automobile if the trains are not running. However, rail strikes are usually scheduled for specific days and travelers can plan around them.

Rail Station Roulette

When railway travel got its start in Britain, London responded by building rail stations—lots of them—all over the city. There is no Grand Central Station in London. Instead, the traveler is faced with more than a dozen major train stations scattered around town. Like the spokes on a wheel, the rail lines from each station reach out and serve different parts of Britain. Major stations include:

- Paddington
- Marylebone
- Euston
- St. Pancras International
- King's Cross
- Liverpool Street
- Fenchurch Street
- Blackfriars
- Charing Cross
- Stratford
- Cannon Street
- London Bridge
- Waterloo and Waterloo East
- Victoria

With the exception of St. Pancras and King's Cross, which are right across the street from each other, getting from one station to another can be a challenge. The Tube is not practical if you are carrying much luggage, and the new Crossrail (Elizabeth Line) only connects a few mainline stations. London's bus system indirectly connects rail stations, but this is not ideal either. Taxis, or taxi-like services, are probably the best way to get between rail stations in London. Try to avoid rush hours because whatever conveyance you choose—bus, taxi, or Tube—getting around town takes longer when London's streets are jammed.

Does train travel to and from London sound like a logistical nightmare? Fortunately, most tourists will probably use only one or two rail stations, either to get into London from an airport or to take a day trip outside the city. Heathrow Airport trains use Paddington rail station and most Gatwick Airport trains use Victoria station. Eurostar trains leave from St. Pancras International. Trains to Hogwarts, as we've already established, leave from King's Cross. Rail services can change, so check the National Rail website at www.nationalrail.co.uk

Finding Harry Potter

Harry Potter fans know that the Hogwarts Express departs from Platform Nine $^3/_4$ inside King's Cross station. But of course there is no such platform...at least one that most of us can see. Instead, there is a retail store filled with Potter merchandise. Just outside there is a photo op platform—complete with a luggage cart embedded in the brick wall. Scenes from Harry Potter movies were filmed in King's Cross while exterior scenes were filmed at St. Pancras station across the street.

Warner Brothers Studio Tour

But you don't have to settle for a mere King's Cross retail store if your family is on the trail of Harry Potter in London. To take a tour of the studios where the Harry Potter films were produced, board a train at Euston rail station for the twenty-minute trip north to Watford Junction rail station. Then take a fifteen-minute connecting bus to the Warner Brothers Studio Tour. In Britain, this is about as close as you can get to stepping foot into the world of Harry Potter, with movie sets recreating Hogwarts' Great Hall, Diagon Alley, the Forbidden Forest, and a full-sized Hogwarts Express.

Most of the venue is wheelchair accessible. There are cafés, a coat/bag check, and toilets onsite. It should come as no surprise that there are multiple gift shops scattered throughout and plenty of opportunities to spend money on Harry Potter merchandise. This is a popular destination, so book tickets in advance.

Website: www.wbstudiotour.co.uk

Making Plans for London

When to Go

A Method to Your Trip Planning Madness

Finding a Hotel

Food, Glorious Food

When to Go

Don't you just love this section in the typical guidebook? Parents with school-age children generally cannot go to London in September or October even though the weather may be beautiful. And most kids would throw a fit if the family decided to pack up and go to London for Christmas or another important holiday. "What about the presents? How will Santa Claus find me?" So yes, it's great to contemplate going at some other time of year, but most overseas families will travel to London during June, July, or August.

Is there any way for visitors to travel in the summer but avoid the crowds? One tip is to plan around the times when British schools are on summer break. British schools usually get out for the summer in early to mid-July, whereas North American school years generally end in June. This gives American families a window of opportunity for travel. During this period you will still encounter crowds, but not the crush that can occur during midsummer. Summertime crowding in London often hits a peak in August when tourists swarm into the city.

Visitors to London will feel the midsummer crunch on the plane trip over. At the airport, clearing border control and picking up baggage can take quite a while. And at major tourist attractions in the city, lines can be notoriously long.

Some airlines hike fares for peak summer travel beginning in mid-June, so those who can begin a trip before the rates go up may save on airfare. But airlines sometimes offer summer sales. This can be a dilemma. If you wait too long to book tickets, all the flights may be filled. But if you book too early you risk missing a summer sale. With today's air travel market, it is almost impossible to predict ticket prices.

Hotel rooms can be less expensive in summer, especially at hotels that cater mainly to business travelers. Families may find summer price breaks at London's business hotels and weekend rates can also be lower than mid-week. That's a good thing, because London hotel rates are expensive by any standard.

Holidays

Here is a list of the major public holidays observed in Britain:
- New Year's Day—January 1. If the date falls on a weekend, the bank holiday is the next weekday.
- Good Friday—varies
- Easter Monday—varies
- Early May Bank Holiday—first Monday in May
- Spring Bank Holiday—last Monday in May
- Summer Bank Holiday—last Monday in August
- Christmas Day—December 25. If the date falls on a weekend, the bank holiday is the next weekday after Boxing Day.
- Boxing Day—December 26

Bank holiday is a quaint term designating an official holiday when banks and some businesses are closed. Be sure to check whether the tourist attractions you want to visit are open on a holiday. Many are closed around Christmas and New Year's, but open on other holidays.

Weather

Britain in summertime means that you can expect the following weather conditions: warm, hot, cool, cold, sunny, cloudy, and wet. Sometimes these all occur in one day! You can look up average temperatures and rainfall, but remember, these are just averages. Use the averages as a guide, but pack something to wear if you encounter abnormal temperatures. With global climate change, there has been a trend toward summer heat waves in London and southern England.

As the summer solstice approaches in June, the days get long—really long—at this latitude. Twilight lasts past 10:00 p.m. in London, and as you travel north to the English Lake District or Scotland there is still light in the western sky at 11:30 p.m. This gives summer visitors extra hours of sightseeing time. Longer days don't necessarily mean extended opening times for tourist attractions, but you can use the longer daylight hours for outdoor activities. British Summer Time (daylight savings time) starts on the last Sunday of March and ends on the last Sunday of October.

A Method to Your Trip Planning Madness

It is amazing how many families do almost no research before taking an overseas trip. At times this method works fine, but serendipitous tourists may miss some great experiences simply because they did not have enough information before arriving in London.

A solution? If you have the luxury of time, start planning six months in advance. Buy or borrow every guidebook you can find (borrow others, *buy* this one). Consider letting your children help plan the trip. Divide the books among family members and start reading. Take notes about things of interest, then swap books and take more notes. Go online and search for sites related to travel, tourism, dining, events, and lodging in London. Browse VisitLondon.com, the city's tourism website, for information. Give kids a map and let them mark points of interest. Encourage kids to read some British children's literature, especially stories that take place in areas you will visit.

When you and your children cannot read another guidebook, website, Sherlock Holmes or Paddington Bear story, it's time for a family conference. Everyone can contribute from their notes as the family begins to develop a master list of places and things to see and do. Narrowing your list down to a trip plan is step two—and this is no small challenge. At this point, independent travelers will begin contacting airlines and hotels directly. People who find this prospect daunting may decide it is time to ask a travel agent for help.

Travel Agents and Trip Insurance

If you are using a travel agent, be sure to pick one with extensive, recent travel experience about London. Any travel agent can sell packaged tours, but it takes knowledge for an agent to answer questions about specific hotels, activities, and other aspects of a trip. Beware of anyone—travel agent or guidebook writer—who strongly steers you toward a particular hotel, airline, car rental agency, and the like. They could be providing their best impartial advice, or they may have an ulterior economic motive.

It is wise to use agents who are members of groups like the American Society of Travel Agents, the Association of British Travel Agents, the Association of Canadian Travel Agencies, or similar organizations. These groups promote ethics in the industry and provide travelers with recourse if they have a complaint about member agents.

Consider purchasing travel/trip insurance when planning a vacation, with or without a travel agent. Keep in mind that trip insurance has its limitations, often buried in pages of small print, and adds to the cost of a vacation. Insurance can be purchased as part of a travel package or independently. And some credit cards include limited travel insurance coverage. For anyone who travels frequently, an annual travel insurance plan may be the best deal.

Laying Out an Itinerary

You have read extensively, taken copious notes, and bookmarked lots of Internet sites. Brochures and guidebooks are piled on the dining room table. How to organize all this information into a trip plan? Lay out the days of your trip in calendar form, with room to list interesting events and places you want to visit. Here are some ideas to keep in mind as you plan your itinerary:

- Fill in anything that is fixed, such as arrival and departure dates and times. If you have pre-purchased theater tickets, add the show times to the calendar. Add any special one-time events you wish to attend.

- Plan for variety by mixing and matching types of activities. Don't put all the museums on one day and all the parks on another. The wise parent carefully intersperses kid-friendly activities with more adult (possibly kid-boring) events.

- Allow plenty of time for each location or activity. You may want to devote more or less time at any spot, but when planning, err on the side of leaving extra time. And remember, it takes time to get from place to place.

- Consider geography. Arrange the days logically, grouping places and events that are reasonably close together on the same day. Plot the itinerary on a map. If routes between sites look like a web spun by a drunken spider, you may want to rearrange your plans.

- Be flexible. Have some backup ideas in case it rains on the day you plan to visit a park or if the lines at some popular destinations are too long.

- Be realistic. As a rule of thumb, when traveling with children, a family can probably manage three major activities a day: one each in the morning, afternoon, and evening. Much more than that and you risk exhausting your kids and yourself.

- Plotting out your itinerary like this is the best way we know to get a handle on your trip plan. Of course, once something is written down, you will likely change it several times before leaving for London, and several times once you are there.

Don't Leave Home Without It

As your plans firm up, we suggest creating a file that includes:
- Your day-by-day itinerary
- Copies of the photograph page from passports (if you lose a passport, the copy will speed up the replacement time)
- Hotel reservation confirmations
- Records of airline tickets, theater tickets, museum passes, rental car reservations
- Phone numbers or websites to report lost credit cards

This information can easily be stored on a tablet or smartphone. But if you are still living in the paper world, print this out. Just how valuable is a trip file? It has saved our vacation when we were faced with a balky hotel, airline, or car rental reservation. If you encounter "Sorry, we have no record of that," you can reply, "Well, as you can see from my copy of your email confirmation here...."

Events

Events, big and small, planned and serendipitous, can make a trip special. It's good to include special events in your itinerary. But be flexible enough to enjoy those unplanned moments when events find you.

On one trip, we had arranged far in advance for tickets to the Ceremony of the Keys at the Tower of London. What we didn't know until we arrived in London was that we were attending the ceremony on the same night as a celebration at nearby Tower Bridge. After the solemn keys ceremony, we ran to the Thames embankment and watched spectacular fireworks above Tower Bridge. That was serendipity at its best.

Seasonal events can enhance your family's London experience. In warm weather months, take advantage of concerts in parks and other outdoor events. But Londoners don't completely retreat inside during

the winter. Temporary ice-skating rinks pop up around the city from November through January, and lights and decorations along major shopping streets draw shoppers and tourists outside.

The publication *Time Out London* has up-to-date information on events and activities.

Finding a Hotel

"Going to London?" said the strange boy,
when Oliver had concluded.

"Yes."

"Got any lodgings?"

"No."

"Money?"

"No."

The strange boy whistled; and put his arms into his
pockets as far as the big coat sleeves would let them go.

"Don't fret your eyelids on that score,"
said the young gentleman.

—*Oliver Twist* by Charles Dickens

When considering where to stay in London, check as many sources as possible. Read through guidebooks and scour websites to locate accommodations in central London. Find a great place? What does the AA (British Automobile Association) guide or website say? Go online again and see what people are writing on travel message boards or services like TripAdvisor. Hotel websites are biased, but they provide photographs of the hotel, maps showing its exact location, and other useful information. Remember, a "palace" to one person may be a "pigsty" to someone else. Do not rely on any one source when deciding where to stay, lest you end up sleeping in a pigsty, or worse.

Even with many sources of information, families traveling to London face several challenges in locating suitable lodging. We have some suggestions, but no outright solutions, to finding:

- Family accommodations
- A quiet, comfortable place to stay
- A convenient location
- Something you can afford

Family Rooms

The typical American hotel room includes two double beds, a full bathroom, and air-conditioning. A family of two adults and one or two children can usually fit into this configuration, perhaps with a rollaway bed for one child. It's not paradise, especially for the parents, but it suffices. For a few dollars more, a traveling family can stay at an all-suite hotel.

This model rarely applies to London's hotel industry, so it is sometimes difficult to find modern family accommodations in the city. One possibility is to try a familiar brand hotel such as a Holiday Inn, Hilton, or Marriott. Kids sometimes stay for free in chain hotels. Some budget hotel chains, such as Premier Inn and Holiday Inn Express, also offer American–style accommodations. There are Premier Inns across the city, including properties at County Hall next to the London

Eye, near Tower Bridge, and adjacent to Victoria rail station. Triple, quad, or family rooms do exist in some London hotels. Check with the individual hotel before reserving a room.

Take a moment to learn the euphemisms employed in the British hotel industry. "Traditional" often means old, a "tourist class hotel" is a lower-grade property, and "first class" is not necessarily top of the line. Modifiers are sometimes used to denote middle-range hotels, so you may see a "moderate first-class" hotel or a "superior tourist class" property.

Quiet Please

Even though locating an air-conditioned hotel in London is sometimes a challenge, your family will probably want air-conditioning during a summer visit. The reason for air-conditioning is noise control. London is a very busy city and closed windows keep out some noise. In warm weather, without air-conditioning, hotel guests must choose between stuffy rooms or noisy rooms. The need for quiet is one reason to check out newer hotel chains. Their construction tends to include double-glazed windows, carpeting, some sound insulation, and quieter plumbing.

You may not share our preference for modern hotels. If you like small, older hotels or B&Bs, you might find something suitable, but it will take research. Sometimes lodging guidebooks associate "quiet" with "no children allowed." For families, quiet means the possibility of a good night's sleep, not the quiet of a nursing home.

Of course, nothing guarantees a quiet hotel or B&B. Ever notice that other hotel guests seem to practice slamming their room doors after 11:00 p.m.? It is these same people who think that a hotel hallway is a fine place to hold loud, protracted conversations late at night or first thing in the morning.

Locate a London hotel on a detailed map for clues about potential road and traffic noise. A hotel facing busy Piccadilly or Kensington Road is going to be exposed to more traffic noise than some place a block off the main artery. No guarantees here, because the hotel could be right next to the Party All Night Pub or some equally loud venue. Google Maps street view is a good way to take a virtual stroll around the neighborhood before booking a hotel. Unfortunately, there may be an inverse relationship between a quiet hotel and one with a central location.

Location, Location, Location

London has good public transportation, so getting from a distant hotel to the major tourist attractions is certainly possible. But do you really want to spend valuable vacation time traveling on the Tube, with children in tow, during the morning or evening rush hour? If your budget allows, wouldn't it be better to stay near some of the sights you want to see? This distinction escapes many experts who advise tourists to look for reasonably priced lodgings in some remote areas of London. As a general rule we recommend staying within a two-and-one-half-mile radius of Buckingham Palace. Many major tourist attractions fall in this central area.

Just about two miles northwest of Buckingham Palace, the **Paddington/Bayswater** area has many tourist-class accommodations and midrange hotels. Bayswater is known for its multi-cultural restaurants and shops, but some of this area is far from major tourist attractions, so visitors must rely on public transportation. Paddington is convenient for people arriving and departing from Heathrow Airport. The Paddington rail station is the London terminus for the Heathrow Express and it is also served by Crossrail/Elizabeth Line trains. If rail transportation to the airport is critical, consider the Hilton Hotel connected to Paddington rail station.

At the southern edge of this area, busy Bayswater Road runs along the top of Kensington Gardens and Hyde Park. Familiar chains? There is a Doubletree hotel and a Hilton hotel on Bayswater Road near the Diana Memorial Playground. Rooms not facing Bayswater Road are probably quieter.

To the west in **Notting Hill** there are few hotels, but it is a popular area for short-term apartment rentals.

In **Knightsbridge and Kensington** you can find many hotels. This area is convenient for visiting Kensington Palace as well as the

Science, Natural History, and Victoria and Albert museums. Major thoroughfares like Brompton/Cromwell Road are extremely busy with accompanying traffic noise. But there are hotels on some quieter side streets, such as the four-star Millennium London Gloucester Hotel.

A bit further west of Kensington/Knightsbridge is **Earl's Court**, a neighborhood with many mid-priced lodgings. Tour companies often book budget travelers in these hotels, and the quality varies. But Earl's Court is farther away from most tourist sights than Bayswater.

Trendy **Chelsea** is home to B&Bs, a few large upscale hotels, and some high-end boutique properties. The five-star Draycott Hotel is an example of Chelsea's small top-tier hotels. Lovely as it is, there few major tourist destinations in Chelsea.

The **Victoria** area is within walking distance of Buckingham Palace. This neighborhood includes downscale hotels as well as nicer spots, so choose carefully. The Goring, a small luxury hotel, is a fashionable choice for families with deep pockets. Rubens at the Palace is another popular hotel in this area, and there is also a budget-level Premier Inn nearby.

It would be nice to stay in **Westminster**, close to the abbey and Parliament. Unfortunately, there are few hotels in this part of London because real estate here is costly. One exception is the moderately priced Sanctuary House Hotel just south of St. James's Park. The upscale Conrad St. James, and St. Ermin's hotels are nearby.

Across the river from Parliament and next door to the **London Eye**, you will find a moderately priced Premier Inn along with an expensive Marriott and a pair of Park Plaza hotels.

The ritzy **St. James's** area is also within walking distance of Buckingham Palace. The hotels in this area are among the most expensive in the city. The luxury Sofitel St. James's is in one of London's prime locations. The Stafford Hotel is tucked into a quiet St. James's side street and offers posh accommodations befitting the area. St. James's is often lumped with its northern neighbor Mayfair as a locale for upscale accommodations.

Mayfair is one of the most convenient areas in London, but convenience comes at a price. Legendary hotels like Brown's, Claridge's, and the Dorchester call Mayfair home. There are a few chain hotels here which are still expensive, just not outrageously so. A popular midrange choice is the Holiday Inn Mayfair, near the over-the-top London Ritz. A few blocks north, the Chesterfield Mayfair Hotel offers luxury, although not at Ritz prices.

Covent Garden is east of Mayfair. This neighborhood is close to West End theaters and attractions around Covent Garden Market, so it has its share of traffic and late-night noise. The popular Fielding Hotel is nearby, and the top-ranked Savoy is a five-minute walk away.

The **City of London** is primarily a financial district, but it has a number of hotels within walking distance of tourist attractions. There is a midrange Club Quarters near St. Paul's Cathedral and a Novotel north of the Tower of London.

There are some modern hotels just south of the Thames near the **Tower of London**, including a Premier Inn on Tower Bridge Road and a Hilton on Tooley Street.

Further east, there are midlevel hotels around the **ExCel Centre** and London City Airport—including offerings from Premier Inn, Novotel, Ibis, and Aloft. Hotels in this area can be less expensive, except during special events at the ExCel center.

Bloomsbury is near the British Museum, the Dickens Museum and Coram's Fields. Bloomsbury offers a number of hotels such as the mid-priced Radisson Edwardian and the upscale Montague on the Gardens.

The **Marylebone** area is just south of Regent's Park. The luxurious Langham Hotel and the exclusive Chiltern Firehouse Hotel are in Marylebone, along with a plethora of other properties. Marylebone is convenient to shopping along Oxford Street, and it has good access to the Tube.

Anyone who has a late-night arrival or an early-morning departure from **Heathrow** or **Gatwick** airports might consider staying at an airport hotel rather than making the commute to and from town. A high-end Sofitel is attached to Heathrow's Terminal 5, ultra convenient for British Airways transatlantic flights. Heathrow's Terminal 4 has a Hilton. For those who aren't claustrophobic, there is also a Yotel short-term "capsule hotel" in Terminal 4. At Gatwick Airport's south terminal, there is a BLOC Hotel, a Hilton, and another diminutive Yotel. The north terminal offers a Hampton, a Sofitel, and a Premier Inn. Some other properties that call themselves "airport hotels" are not actually at the airports and require shuttle bus rides from the terminals.

But who are we kidding? Official statistics are hard to find, but a recent survey estimated that there are more than 139,000 hotel rooms in London.

And That Will Be £450, Plus VAT and Service Charges

We promised to address four issues at the start of this section, and we have delivered on the first three: we've discussed family accommodations, given some hints on getting a quiet hotel room, and provided an overview of hotel locations. That leaves the last issue—finding affordable places to stay. It is tempting to skip this subject because of one simple fact: lodging in London is expensive. Lodging that meets all the criteria we have outlined is both expensive *and* difficult to find. There are no magical answers, but here are some suggestions.

Never Say Never

Never accept the published hotel rate at a large city hotel. You will always qualify for some lower rate: weekend packages, honeymoon packages (kind of hard to explain when you're traveling with kids, but worth a try), government rates, corporate rates, automobile association rates, senior citizen rates, advance purchase rates, special rates for people paying with a particular credit card . . . *something*. If nothing else works and you are planning to stay at a chain hotel, at least collect points by joining the chain's frequent guest program.

Like most large cities, London has many hotels that cater primarily to business travelers and these hotels may have lower rates on weekends. You can also take advantage of off-peak rates at business-oriented London hotels. Happily, off-peak for business travel includes July and August, which is exactly when many families visit London on vacation.

Call Around

Sometimes it is possible to snag low rates by calling a hotel directly. Take this a step further and compare rates quoted by the hotels, their corporate reservations centers, and websites. Bidding on a travel auction site, or using a reveal-the-name-after-you-book site, are also ways to obtain lower-cost accommodations. But travel auctions are not for everyone. It can be difficult to arrange family rooms, adjoining rooms, or any special configurations using these sites.

Be sure to compare apples to apples. Are the rooms the same? Some hotels have several grades of accommodations, including both refurbished rooms and shabby rooms. Does the quoted rate include:

- Value added tax (it should)
- Service charges
- Breakfasts (for the whole family or just two adults)

Make sure that the rates are quoted on the same basis: per room, per night. Do children stay free? If so, are there age limits? Finally, understand whether the rate is quoted in pounds, dollars, or euros. This advice sounds basic, but if you don't determine this in advance, you could be in for a nasty surprise.

Quality Ratings

Sherlock Holmes would have been comfortable searching for a decent place to stay in London, applying his powers of inductive reasoning, using his able assistant Watson, and examining clues under a magnifying glass. Holmes would have made a terrific trip planner because he seemed to have a lot of free time and no money worries.

Fortunately, some of the detective work has already been done by England's official tourist organization (Visit England), and one of its largest travel organizations (the Automobile Association). These groups rate thousands of hotels, B&Bs, and other lodging establishments. They use a rating system that awards one to five stars based on standards of quality, services, and facilities.

The more stars, the better the hotel or B&B. A hotel is graded with an emphasis on its facilities—for example, bathrooms, elevators, and room service. To qualify for one star, a hotel must offer all en suite or private baths. Two-star hotels must hit a higher quality standard. The three-star level includes things like room service and public area Wi-Fi. As for toting your suitcases to your room, even a one-star hotel must offer help with luggage, although lifts/elevators to all floors are not required until the five-star level. Even around-the-clock hot water isn't necessary to qualify for a two-star hotel rating in Britain! Amazingly, only five-star hotels are expected to offer air-conditioned rooms. From

an American perspective, where inexpensive hotels usually come with air-conditioning and elevators, it is a little disconcerting to read these standards. *No hot water after 10:00 p.m.?* Well, tourist, you're not in Kansas anymore.

For B&Bs and other non-hotels, the star ratings differ a bit. For example, at the four-star level, at least half of a B&B's rooms must have private baths. A five-star B&B must provide fans in guest rooms during hot weather. With these standards at the upper end, it doesn't take much to imagine the realities of lower rated establishments.

Take the ratings systems with a grain of salt. One of the nicest places we stayed in Britain was a beautiful B&B in the tiny west coast village of Crackington Haven. The owners had dropped out of the official inspection program, claiming that it emphasized facilities at the expense of quality.

The Flat Alternative

Families staying in London for more than a few days may want to consider renting an apartment (a "flat") as an alternative to staying in a hotel. Flats come in all sizes and quality levels. The better ones can cost as much as a good hotel room, but there are less expensive options too. What a flat offers families is more space and kitchen facilities. Fixing a few family meals in a flat is cheaper than eating every meal in a restaurant.

Many rental flats are located in residential areas away from major tourist destinations.

Some factors to consider:

- Is this a legitimate rental and is the landlord/rental company reputable?
- Is a deposit required? How will you make payment?
- Is the flat air-conditioned? Not many are.
- Is the building new, renovated, or "classic"?
- On what floor is the flat located? In Britain, as in much of Europe, floors are labeled starting with ground, then first, second, etc. So a British first floor is an American second floor.
- Are there lifts (elevators)?
- How convenient is the flat to what you want to see in London? Is it near a Tube stop?
- What is the neighborhood like?

Online rental services such as Airbnb and HomeAway have opened up some lower cost rental options throughout London. There are also traditional companies specializing in London flat rentals. Renting a flat while on vacation is a matter of choice. Do you want to mingle with the natives, shop for food, and fix meals? Do you have the time to devote to domestic chores during your visit?

B&Bs

The term *bed and breakfast* covers a lot of ground. It applies both to families that rent out one or two bedrooms in their homes and to larger establishments that are essentially small hotels. But virtually all B&Bs share one characteristic: the ubiquitous English breakfast.

At any B&B, charm is a subjective factor. It varies from "working-class spare bedroom" to "country squire's luxury townhouse." It takes some detective work to determine a location's charm factor sight unseen. Check guidebooks, social media and sites like TripAdvisor. But beware of falsified reviews. Note that B&B prices are sometimes quoted per person, not per room. Children generally do not stay for free.

Sleep well!

Food, Glorious Food

Food, glorious food! Hot sausage and mustard!
While we're in the mood—Cold jelly and
custard! Peas, pudding and saveloys!
What next is the question?
Rich gentlemen have it, boys—In-di-gestion!
—*Oliver!* lyrics by Lionel Bart

Meals can be a real challenge. That's a fact of life for parents traveling with children. And the price of dining out in London can be expensive. Fortunately, London has more dining choices than ever before.

Full English Breakfast

If you're lucky, breakfast is included with your hotel room. All B&Bs include breakfast—that's the reason for the second B. And many hotels include breakfast, too. Breakfasts come in two basic varieties: continental and full English. For kids who normally survive on cereal, continental breakfast may suffice. The full English breakfast is a heavy tradition. Heavy on fried eggs, heavy on bacon and sausage, heavy on toast and jam. And as a bonus, the full English breakfast may come with broiled mushrooms and broiled tomatoes. Not that there is anything nutritionally wrong with mushrooms or tomatoes, but the first time they are served at breakfast, non-British parents should be prepared for strange looks or inappropriate comments from their children. Sometimes, the breakfast includes baked beans as a side dish. This is the point where many overseas visitors draw the line in the cultural sand.

The Brown Bag Solution

One solution for feeding the family is to go on a picnic. If the weather is good, head for Hyde Park, Green Park, St. James's Park, Regent's Park . . . you get the idea. In central London, there is a sandwich shop on almost every corner. These work well for families in search of a quick meal. Costa and Pret a Manger are chains with fresh, reasonably priced lunchtime fare. Most patrons carry out food, but there are tables for those who wish to stay and eat. One advantage to carryout ("takeaway") is that cold carryout food is exempt from the hefty value added tax.

Teatime

"At any rate I'll never go THERE again!" said Alice as she picked her way through the wood. "It's the stupidest tea-party I ever was at in all my life!"

—*Alice's Adventures in Wonderland* by Lewis Carroll

Tea is not just a drink in England. It is a quintessential dining and social experience. Tea comes in all varieties, costs, and degrees of formality. If your children have the patience, book a table for afternoon tea. Otherwise, find a less formal spot to enjoy teatime.

Afternoon tea generally consists of tea, scones with jam and clotted cream, pastries or cake, and perhaps even delicate sandwiches. There is nothing low fat or low cholesterol about it. Will kids like it? Probably, and you can always order something else if they do not drink hot tea.

Many London hotels offer afternoon tea. Some—like the upscale Ritz, Four Seasons, and Brown's—are famous for over-the-top tea extravaganzas. But the average Londoner hardly has the time or the inclination for this level of daily tea ritual.

Pub Grub and Other Choices

So far we have covered breakfast, lunch, and tea. What about dinner? Some travel experts advise that pub food is a good bet because it is cheap and filling. To be blunt, some traditional pub food can sound unappetizing to children. However, today's pubs are as likely to serve cheeseburgers and ice cream as they are to offer bangers and spotted dick. You can probably find something on the menu that will please your children.

London has a massive number of ethnic restaurants. This is good news if your kids like Asian, Indian, or Italian food. You can enjoy appetizing, reasonably priced meals in some of the city's ethnic establishments. It is also possible to find overpriced, uninspired food here.

With most children, you cannot go wrong with plain pizza, but the trick in London is to track down kid-friendly pizza. Cheese-and-tomato pizza sometimes features tomato slices instead of tomato sauce. We've even seen curry pizza. Pizza Express and Ask are popular London chains offering pizza and other Italian dishes. Celebrity chef Jamie Oliver oversees the Jamie's Italian chain of midscale restaurants with several London locations.

Food trucks and seasonal pop-up restaurants offer quick food options. Walking along the south bank of the Thames, what could be cooler than buying frozen yogurt from a converted double-decker London bus? Or fish tacos from a refitted 1960s Volkswagen van?

Informal, cafeteria-style food is served at some London churches, museums, and historical sites. Here are a few examples:

- The Crypt Café at St. Martin-in-the-Fields
- The café in the Victoria and Albert Museum (the first museum restaurant in the world)
- The cafeteria in the basement of Central Hall Westminster, right across the street from Westminster Abbey
- The New Armouries Café on the grounds of the Tower of London

Wagamama, the ubiquitous noodle chain, offers inexpensive and fresh Asian-inspired noodle dishes in locations throughout London. Coffee shops are everywhere in central London. Starbucks, yes, but others too, like Caffé Nero, Costa Coffee, and local outlets trying to survive in a corporate coffee culture. Be aware that some London restaurants do not open for dinner until 7:00 or 7:30 p.m. Fortunately, London has a number of chain restaurants that serve dinner earlier. In this case, the term *chain restaurant* does not mean fast-food places like McDonald's or Burger King, although you will find these in London. We're referring to real sit-down restaurants like Bella Italia, Giraffe, Café Rouge, and Carluccio's. These places are informal and reasonable by London standards. Best of all, you don't have to wait until 7:30 p.m. to feed the family.

On Your Way to London

Did You Forget Anything?

Passports

Most foreign visitors need a valid passport to enter Britain. As of this writing, US, Commonwealth, and European Union citizens do not need a visa. Passports are required for the whole family, and children of all ages must have their own passports. Even with a passport, there are strict requirements for international travel by children when both parents do not accompany them. Travel restrictions can come as a surprise when one parent, or a grandparent, tries to take a child on an overseas trip. Generally, it is best to have a notarized letter, signed by both parents, with specific consent to travel.

Check the State Department's website at www.travel.state.gov for more on the US passport process. See the Passport Canada website at www.ppt.gc.ca for information on Canadian passports.

Luggage

From the carpet-bag she took out seven flannel night-gowns, four cotton ones, a pair of boots, a set of dominoes, two bathing-caps and a postcard album. Last of all came a folding camp-bedstead with blankets and eider-down complete, and this she set down between John's cot and Barbara's.

—*Mary Poppins* by P. L. Travers

We enjoy planning and taking trips, but we dislike packing and transporting luggage. Short trips of a week or less are not too bad, but it is a challenge to pack for an extended family vacation. The best way

to pack for a summertime trip to London? Plan a layered wardrobe: short-sleeved shirts over which you can put a sweater and a water-repellent jacket.

The more you pack the heavier the luggage becomes, and not every child can lift a heavy suitcase. Wheeled suitcases are your friends, but try out luggage before you travel. Tippy suitcases are no fun when you are running to catch a train or an elevator. And there are times on a trip when you will have to lift the suitcases, so make sure that you can manage your bags. Most kids are adept at carrying a heavy backpack to school, so consider using backpacks as part of your family luggage. Small backpacks work well as airplane carry-ons and they can be used for picnics and hiking excursions during the trip.

Airline baggage allowances and restrictions are a major consideration. The allowances vary by airline and ticket class. Be aware that European measurements defining carry-on luggage sizes are smaller than American carry-on measurements.

As every seasoned traveler knows, busy airports are full of look-alike bags, so mark your bags creatively. Use suitcase locks approved by the US Transportation Security Administration (TSA). UK security screeners also accept these locks.

Raingear

In case you haven't heard, it rains in London. A lot. Consider using nontoxic waterproof spray on shoes, jackets and coats, hats, backpacks, and your children. On second thought, don't waterproof the kids, but do spray just about everything else. This will come in handy if it rains. Plus, if you go to all this effort, it probably won't rain one drop.

Not that obsessive? Well, at least consider lightweight rain jackets for the family. Of course, if it rains you could buy those garish, cheap plastic ponchos from a souvenir vendor in London. But that brings us to the next tip...

Blending In

You may be a tourist in London, but you don't have to look like one. Londoners sport all varieties of fashion, but few of them dress or act like stereotypical tourists. Constantly taking photographs? Studying the maps on your phone while standing in the middle of a crowded sidewalk? Wearing a t-shirt advertising your favorite brand of beer? Sure signs of being a tourist.

Cultural stereotypes are problematic, but one characteristic often associated with tourists is loudness. And failure to use correct local terminology is another faux pas. Asking for directions to "the bathroom" instead of using the British terms *loo* and *toilet* marks you as a sure tourist. On the other hand, don't go overboard and adopt a fake British accent—Londoners will know you are not a native.

Recording Memories

Cameras

Before leaving on your trip, make sure your phone/camera is working properly. Finding out that a device is malfunctioning is an unwelcome surprise during or after a vacation. If you are taking a digital camera, or using your phone to take pictures, be sure you have enough free memory to store lots of photos. Think twice before uploading gigabytes of photos and video while data roaming.

Postcards, Scrapbooks, and Journals

As a family activity, mail yourselves a postcard from London. Buy a postcard showing a favorite London site and write a note to yourselves about what a wonderful trip you are having. Then find a mailbox—only an old-fashioned red postbox will do—and take a photograph of your children as they mail the postcard home. When you get back from vacation, the postcard and the photo will be great additions to a scrapbook.

A trip to London gives kids ample opportunity to collect things: ticket stubs from trains and theaters, and brochures from hotels and tourist information counters. Relax your parental tendency to throw away all this junk. Let your children collect items as a record of the trip. Intersperse this collected material with photographs, and you will have the makings of a memorable family keepsake.

Another way to record the trip is to take along travel journals for every family member. Of course you can do this online if everyone is carrying their own device. Most school-age children can use practice with their writing skills, and young artists may want to include drawings in their journals. At the end of each day on the trip, take a few minutes to write in the journals. After a busy day of touring, children may have a hard time staying awake long enough to write a few lines. But it is surprising how quickly you can forget the details of a vacation, so a journal can be an important way to help preserve travel memories.

Sights and Sounds

Sightseeing is on every tourist's agenda, but to fully appreciate London be prepared to listen as you tour the city. Some examples:

- Be anywhere close to Big Ben at the top of the hour. Noon and midnight are best...with twelve loud BONGS. If Big Ben is off-line for maintenance, there are plenty of church bells to fill the silence.
- Listen for accents. You will hear a variety of languages and accents, some typical of London natives, some not.
- Listen to the organist practice in Westminster Abbey or stop by a lunchtime concert at St. Martin-in-the-Fields church.

Children can listen for train whistles, station announcements in the Tube, overheard conversations of local children, shouted commands at the changing of the guards—all uniquely local and all a part of their trip memories.

Guardians of the Past

Overseas visitors to England may notice that many historic landmarks are owned or operated by one of two organizations: the National Trust or English Heritage. The Trust is a nonprofit group that preserves historic land, gardens, and buildings. English Heritage is similar, except it receives government support. Each organization operates a different set of properties, but there is some overlap. At Stonehenge, for example, the National Trust owns the land, and English Heritage operates the site.

National Trust

A visitor's pass from one of these groups can save money on admission to historic sites. Neither organization operates many of the major tourist attractions in London, so visitors who are not venturing out of the city may not save enough to justify purchasing a pass.

English Heritage Overseas Visitor Pass

This pass admits visitors into English Heritage sites only, and is good for nine or sixteen days. English Heritage properties in London include the Chapter House in Westminster Abbey, the Jewel Tower near Parliament, and Wellington Arch. Purchase the pass online at www.english-heritage.org.uk or at many English Heritage properties. English Heritage also offers annual memberships.

Royal Oak and National Trust

Americans can join the Royal Oak Foundation, an affiliate of the National Trust. Royal Oak membership includes admission to all Trust properties, and a family membership is a relative bargain. Like English Heritage, the National Trust operates only a few properties in London. But the Trust has partnerships with a number of smaller museums such as the Benjamin Franklin House, and the Foundling Museum. These offer discounts on admission for Trust and Royal Oak members. Information on properties, passes, and memberships can be found on the National Trust website at www.nationaltrust.org.uk and the Royal Oak website at www.royal-oak.org

Historic Royal Palaces Pass

Historic Royal Palaces is the group that runs Hampton Court Palace, Kensington Palace, the Banqueting House, the Tower of London, and Kew Palace. The agency sells passes that admit visitors to several palaces at a savings over individual admission charges. Historic Royal Palaces offers annual memberships including memberships in its American Friends affiliate. Purchase passes and individual tickets online at www.hrp.org.uk

London Pass

The London Pass is a commercial pass that provides admission to many tourist attractions in London. The London Pass is not cheap, so review the list of attractions covered to be certain that you will get your money's worth. To make the card worthwhile, you need to visit a fair number of sites during a relatively short time period. One huge benefit of the London Pass is that pass holders usually get to bypass regular ticket lines. During peak months, that alone may be reason enough to invest in a pass. The London Pass website is www.londonpass.com

The London Pass company also sells a more limited pass covering a handful of key London attractions. You can purchase a one-month pass covering three to seven sites, along with other London sightseeing discounts. Adult and child passes are available. The London Explorer Pass sales website is www.londonexplorerpass.com

The Royal Collection

The Royal Collection operates public openings at Buckingham Palace, the Royal Mews, the Queen's Collection, and Windsor Castle. The Royal Collection does not offer a multi-site pass. But you can get your individual ticket stamped at the end of a visit, and then you can come back repeatedly to the same site for one year.

Keep in mind that many major museums in London offer free admission, so don't buy any pass assuming that you will save money on museum tickets.

Getting There

European visitors to London have the luxury of choice: they can fly, take a train through the English Channel tunnel, or come by ferryboat. Almost everyone else faces a long plane ride. For families traveling with young children, this journey can be a challenge. The trick is keeping the challenge from becoming an ordeal.

Look! It's a Bird, It's an Eight-Hour Plane Ride

Many airlines offer flights from North America to London that leave in the evening and arrive the next morning. Although an overnight flight does mean one less night in a hotel, the plane ride can be tiring for families. A few flights leave in the morning and arrive in London the same evening (London time). This avoids an overnight flight and may reduce the effects of jet lag. Return flights are somewhat easier because they usually leave London in the early afternoon and, flying with the sun, arrive in North America later that same day. Either way, it is a long ride.

Here are some survival tips for families flying overnight from the American East Coast to London. These tips can be adjusted for longer flights.

Consider eating dinner before boarding. Once airborne, decline the meal on the plane. This may earn some funny looks from flight attendants, but if you eat dinner on the plane at 8:00 or 9:00 p.m. US Eastern Time, you'll be offered breakfast just four hours later as the plane approaches the United Kingdom. Out-of-sync meal schedules contribute to jet lag.

On the flight over, try to adjust to a London schedule as soon as possible. One strategy is to set your watch to London time when you get on the plane. Wow, it's midnight already, time to go to sleep. Okay, it is really 2:00 a.m. US Eastern Time when the plane arrives in London and you probably got no sleep. But convince yourself it was a normal night or risk falling asleep soon after landing.

Once in London, try to follow a normal schedule. You will be tired, but don't take a nap, unless naps are still a part of your child's daily schedule. Eat meals at regular London times and try to stay awake until at least 9:00 p.m. In theory, by the next day you will have adjusted to London time. Good luck with this routine, particularly if traveling with young children.

Motion Sickness and Ear Pain

If your child is prone to motion sickness, be prepared before you get on the plane. Check with a pediatrician about whether the child can safely take motion sickness medication. Some children have success with pressure point wristbands. If these work for your child, wristbands are a drug-free alternative for preventing motion sickness. Expecting motion sickness to be inevitable while flying with a child? Be prepared for the worst and pack a change of clothes.

On an airplane, changes in air pressure can cause ear pain for children and adults alike. Parents can try giving children something to chew during takeoff and landing, and babies can suck their pacifiers to equalize pressure. You can also buy special earplugs that slowly equalize air pressure. The earplugs also block out some noise, so they have an added benefit when you are trying to sleep on the plane.

Seating Arrangements

Airplane seating has become a not-so-funny joke, as hundreds of passengers are crammed into narrow seats with almost no legroom. A family lucky enough to travel first or business class can sit back, relax, and try to enjoy the flight. Others should read on for some coping tips. Families traveling with children may want to get window seats for the kids, with an adult in the seat next to each child. When it is time to sleep, children can prop a pillow against the cabin wall or lean against Mom or Dad.

Some airlines offer cots for children under age two. These attach to a cabin bulkhead wall and allow the child to lie down. To arrange for this, check with the airline when making reservations. Although airlines may allow an infant to be held in the lap of an adult, we question the safety of this practice and the sanity of anyone who plans to hold a baby for the duration of an overseas plane ride. The lap baby fare is cheap, but buying a separate seat for a baby allows use of an approved child safety seat or harness on board.

Generally, seats over the wings near the center of the plane have a smoother ride than seating near the tail or the nose. Think of a plane as a seesaw—the least motion will be near the center pivot point rather than at the ends. Note to nervous flyers: don't think of an airplane as a seesaw, think of it as a puffy cloud gliding calmly through a bright-blue sky.

Some airlines no longer allow passengers to preselect seat locations. Others do offer seat choices but tend to pile on extra fees. Members of an airline's frequent-flier program may find it easier to preselect seats. Regardless of the airline's stated policy, decide in advance where you want to sit. Let the airline know that you are traveling with children. Request the preferred seat assignment when purchasing tickets and again when checking in for the flight. At the gate, families with young children are sometimes allowed to board first. Listen for the boarding announcement to take advantage of this privilege.

The Class System

Most families purchase coach/economy tickets out of economic necessity and suffer through the indignities of "cattle class." Those fortunate enough to fly business class or first class to London have a much less stressful experience. They enjoy faster check-in, larger baggage allowances, separate departure and arrival lounges, better food, and humanely sized seating. Many airlines offer flatbed seating, where passengers might actually get some sleep on the way to London. Virgin Atlantic calls this "upper class," as if we need reminding that the class system operates in the air.

Recognizing that not everyone can afford to fly business class, some

airlines offer premium economy service. For a moderate increase in ticket price, this class includes more legroom and a slight upgrade in amenities and service. Premium economy can be a good compromise for traveling families who can afford the increased fares.

In-Flight Distractions and Fluffy the Bear

If sleep is impossible on the plane, parents face hours of entertaining restless children. Fortunately, on overseas flights, some airlines provide activity kits for kids. These are good for an hour or so . . . then what?

Let each child carry a small backpack filled with paperback books, small games or toys, a journal or sketchbook, markers and pens, and maybe a stuffed animal. Don't pack expensive items that may get lost on a long trip.

A special note about Fluffy the Bear (or whatever the name/species of your child's favorite). If Fluffy absolutely must go on the trip, plan in advance how to keep track of her. Perhaps Fluffy needs her own identifying luggage tag. Maybe she really would like to "ride" in the suitcase or backpack and come out only at bedtime. Tracking down Fluffy if she gets left in an airport, on the plane, in a taxi, on a train, or in a hotel is not how parents want to spend their travel time and emotional energy!

London's Airports

Most long haul flights arrive at Heathrow Airport, about sixteen miles west of central London, or Gatwick Airport, twenty-eight miles south of downtown.

Getting to central London from Gatwick is easy because there is frequent express train service from the airport to Victoria rail station. The trip takes thirty to forty minutes. Non-express trains take a few minutes longer but cost less. Because London is nearly thirty miles away, taking a taxi from Gatwick to central London is an expensive and lengthy proposition. For more information on Gatwick, check the airport's website at www.gatwickairport.com

Arriving at Heathrow? The size of this airport can be daunting, as are the transportation choices. Heathrow has its own high-speed rail link to Paddington station in downtown London and travel time is about fifteen minutes. Look for Heathrow Express signs in the arrivals area. Non-express Elizabeth Line trains also serve Heathrow and connect to Paddington and other stations in London. Most passengers taking the train from Heathrow to Paddington will require a taxi to complete their journeys. For more information see the Heathrow Express website at www.heathrowexpress.com and the Crossrail/Elizabeth Line website at www.crossrail.co.uk

The London Underground (Tube) also serves Heathrow and provides the least expensive way to reach downtown. But visitors corralling children and luggage might want to avoid the Tube at this point. Reasons? There is little space for luggage, it is crowded during rush hours, transfers are often required, and it is difficult to negotiate stairs in some stations.

A taxi ride from Heathrow to downtown is an expensive, but

reliable option. A reputable airport transfer service can also be a good way to get between the airports and downtown London. Drivers meet visitors at the airport and take them directly to their hotels. Transfer services can be less expensive than genuine London taxis, but they are less strictly regulated, so service levels and prices may vary. Assuming you have an active cell phone when you get to London, you can also use a ride-hailing service for an airport ride. Be sure to check the service's website for information about pickup locations at the airport.

The National Express company operates various bus/coach services from airports to central London and also connections between London's airports. See the National Express website at www.nationalexpress.com for more information.

However, with London's heavy traffic, it is hard for any on-the-road transportation service to beat the express rail services.

Getting Around Town

Which is the way to London Town,

To see the King in his golden crown?

One foot up and one foot down,

That's the way to London Town.

Which is the way to London Town,

To see the Queen in her silken gown?

Left! Right! Left! Right! Up and down,

Soon you'll be in London Town!

Which is the way to London Town?

Over the hills, across the down,

Over the ridges and over the bridges,

That is the way to London Town.

And what shall I see in London Town?

Many a building old and brown.

Many a real, old-fashioned street

You'll be sure to see in London Town.

— Traditional children's rhyme

Finding Your Way

Trivia fans and lost tourists will be interested to read that London is about 600 square miles, filled with more than eight million residents.

In London, the term *street plan* is an oxymoron—there is no plan to London's streets. This city evolved from the streetscape laid down in Roman times. It was abandoned, burned, and rebuilt by Saxons, Normans, and Victorian reformers. It was flattened by Nazi bombs, rebuilt, and modernized. The result? Tourists need a good sense of direction to avoid becoming hopelessly lost. Tiny, foldable pocket maps are easy to carry and inconspicuous. But details are important and most visitors will rely on smartphone maps.

Underground and Bus

Paddington decided the Underground was quite the most exciting thing that had ever happened to him . . . "I shall always travel on this Underground in the future," said Paddington, politely. "I'm sure it's the nicest in all London."

—*A Bear Called Paddington* by Michael Bond

Thank heavens for London's public transportation network because driving in London is a tourist's worst nightmare. By all means, use the Underground (Tube) and bus systems as your primary transport in the city. Commuter rail lines, notably the London Overground, augment the Underground system. The new Elizabeth Line (Crossrail) connects eastern and western London suburbs. Central London Crossrail stations integrate with the Underground and help speed east-west journeys in the city. All these use the same electronic fare card/payment system.

Kids generally enjoy trips on both the Tube and London's red double-decker buses (riding on the top level, in the front seats, of course). But try to avoid rush hours. The crush on the Tube is disconcerting for a six-foot-tall adult—it can be frightening for a four-foot-tall child. Bus travel during rush hours is maddeningly slow in central London.

Transport for London divides the city into travel zones and most of central London tourist attractions are in Zone 1. The zone numbers get higher farther afield. For example, suburban Kew Gardens is in

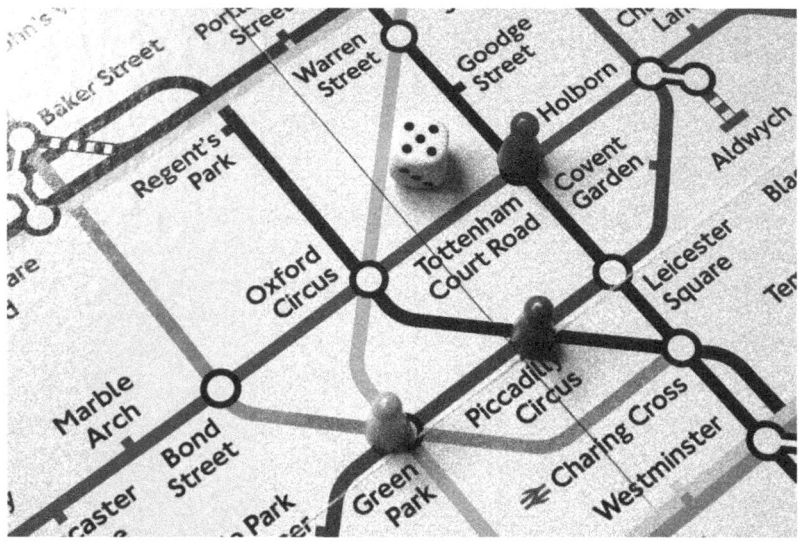

Zone 4. Visitors will want to choose a ticket option based on when they will travel, where they intend to go, and how long they are staying in London.

Transport for London offers a confusing array of tickets and fares. There are individual trip tickets, single and multiday Travelcards, and electronic Oyster cards. Cash purchase of single tickets is the most expensive option. Fares for Oyster card users are generally the lowest and there is a daily price cap on the cards. Oyster cards can be purchased online or in London from Tube stations and other locations including Heathrow airport. Transport for London is also pioneering contactless credit and debit card technology for bus and Underground fares.

Fare options get even more confusing for families who want to take advantage of reduced fares for children. Kids ages eleven to fifteen can get a fourteen-day young visitor discount on an Oyster Card. Apply at Underground station ticket offices and Transport for London Visitor Centres. Or buy a child rate Travelcard instead. Visitors sixteen and older pay adult fares.

So what's the best deal? Visitors who just want convenience and unlimited travel should simply purchase Oyster Cards. Bargain hunters can check the Transport for London website at www.tfl.gov.uk

Here are some tips for traveling on the Tube:

- Google Maps and other smartphone apps include detailed public transportation routes for London, so plan your journeys before departing.

- Don't leave bags or packages sitting unattended. Transport police may suspect a bomb and blow up your bag of souvenirs.

- Have one adult quickly distribute tickets/passes to family members just before boarding a bus or going through the Tube ticket turnstiles. Then collect the tickets and put them in a safe place.

- Touch Oyster cards to the yellow readers in the starting station and also when leaving the destination station.

- Hold children's hands.

- Mind the gap! Everyone's favorite Transport for London phrase, this refers to the gap between the train and the platform at some stops. Be careful!

- Look for electronic signs on platforms that tell how long until the next train arrives and where it is heading. The signs display the final stop of the next train.

- Changing between different Underground lines in a station can often involve a very long walk through connecting passageways.

The advantage of bus travel is that riders can sightsee while journeying around London. But during rush hours, central London buses can slow to a crawl. There are a huge number of bus routes in London, and the maps and information posted at bus stops can be confusing. Use a transportation app or consult the online journey planner on the Transport for London website. You cannot simply hop on a London bus and buy a ticket—you must have an Oyster card, Travelcard, or contactless payment card. Keep in mind that buses generally stop only at marked stops. There are automatic stops and request stops, where you must hail a bus to get on, or indicate that you want to get off.

Taxi!

The driver looked hard at Paddington and then at the inside of his nice, clean taxi. "Bears is sixpence extra," he said, gruffly.

—A Bear Called Paddington by Michael Bond

The black London taxi is as much a symbol of the city as is Tower Bridge or Big Ben. In recent years, the traditional black paint has been replaced by garish advertising on the cabs. We suspect that most parents waiting in the taxi queue hope to get into a traditional black taxicab, while their kids are rooting for the cab bedecked in retro-psychedelic colors.

No matter the color, a real London taxi is a reliable, if expensive, way to get around town. Unlike some cities, where almost anyone with a driver's license can operate a cab, London requires taxi drivers to acquire a detailed understanding of the city's streets and sites. London taxi drivers know where you are going. After a long journey, an overseas visitor's first impression of London might be from the inside of a taxi. Jet-lagged kids wake up fast when they ride in the taxi's rear-facing jump seats and realize they're ON THE WRONG SIDE OF THE ROAD!

London has other taxi-like services. Order a taxi from a hotel, and you may get a private car service or minicab. Be aware that the training of the driver and the condition of the vehicle can vary by car company. Minicabs cannot pick up passengers on the street. You can also use smartphone apps to summon ride-hailing services in London.

A word about costs. London's official taxicabs use a metering system that records time and distance traveled. Some minicabs use meters, but most have set fees. So the laws of economics apply, one of which is: it's easy to take money from tourists. In a taxicab, be wary of the few drivers who will deliberately take longer-than-necessary routes. In a taxi or minicab, get an estimate of the fare before starting a journey. If you are traveling with lots of luggage, make sure the taxi can carry it all. Traditional London taxis can accommodate five people, a couple of big suitcases in the passenger compartment, and a bag or two next to the driver. A limited number of London taxis are Metrocabs, which can carry six or seven passengers. Minicabs and ride-hailing service vehicles may have different passenger capacities and space for baggage.

Finally, one other potential hazard is the so-called taxi tout. Working airports and rail stations, these guys pounce on tourists, carry bags to a car outside, and promise low fares. Two problems: the fares are usually not low and the practice of touting is illegal.

Phones and the Internet

It wasn't often that Paddington made a telephone call—for
one thing he always found it a bit difficult with paws.

—*Paddington Goes to Town* by Michael Bond

Communication has come a long way since the days of the traditional
red London telephone booth. The iconic phone booths still make a
great photo op.

Phone Numbers

London phone numbers are eleven digits long, most begin with the London area code (020), and they look like this:

020 #### ####

But you don't always use all eleven digits. If you are calling within greater London, drop the 020 city code and just use the eight-digit phone number. Call 999 or 112 for emergency fire, police, and ambulance services, and 101 for nonemergency police services.

Calling Britain

To call Britain from the United States or Canada:
- Start with the North American international access code (011)
- Then add the UK country code (44)
- Do *not* use the zero prefix on the British telephone number
- Then add the rest of the phone number
- Example: 011 44 20 7123 4567

To call Britain from a European country:
- Use the European international access code (00)
- Then add the UK country code (44)
- Do *not* use the zero prefix on the British telephone number
- Then add the rest of the phone number
- Example: 00 44 20 7123 4567

Phoning Home

To call the United States or Canada from Britain:
- Begin with the UK international access code (00)
- Then add the US/Canada country code (1)
- Then add the area code and phone number
- Example: 00 1 555 992-1234

Although there are other options available, the best way to call

Britain, or call home, is to use an Internet service like Skype, Google Hangouts, Facetime, or Facebook Messenger.

Mobile Phones

Think twice before you use your smartphone in London. International data roaming and calling rates can be outrageous. Our advice? Make sure your device is unlocked and usable in the UK, then buy a British SIM card and a short-term data plan when you arrive in London. Mobile phone stores sprout like mushrooms at airports and in London shopping areas. There are even SIM card vending machines near some baggage claims at London airports. The downside to purchasing a SIM card in London is that you won't know your cell phone number before you leave on your trip.

Of course, you could buy a SIM card before you leave home, rent an international phone, buy a worldwide data plan, or signup for your provider's overseas roaming plans. But these all seem to cost more than just getting a SIM and data plan once you get to London. Finally, don't forget to pack a plug adapter to charge your devices using British electrical outlets.

Computers and Wi-Fi

Taking computers on a trip is a mixed blessing. Many travelers want or need to stay connected during vacations. But there are some negatives: additional security screening at airports, added weight to pack and carry electronics, and the chance they will be lost or stolen.

Quality London hotels usually offer Wi-Fi in rooms, but they often charge exorbitant fees for getting online. Large swaths of the city are Wi-Fi hot zones and Wi-Fi can be found in many coffee shops, bars, or pubs. But not all of these networks are free.

Medical and Money Matters

Most people would rather not think about getting sick while on a long-planned vacation to London. Money issues can also induce travel angst. In both cases, a little preparedness goes a long way.

Is There a Doctor in the House?

Many insurers will reimburse for emergency medical expenses abroad, but they may require travelers to contact them for authorization. Health insurers can be sticklers about notification. A US or Canadian medical insurance card is probably useless in Britain, but take it anyway, especially if it includes the phone numbers to notify the insurer of a medical emergency. Notice that we said many insurers will *reimburse* eligible expenses. This means you may have to pay out-of-pocket for doctor, pharmacy, or hospital bills in Britain. Before leaving home, check with your health insurance company to find out exactly what coverage your family will have while traveling abroad.

The United Kingdom operates a national health plan. Even tourists can obtain emergency medical treatment through this plan. For most visitors, anything more than emergency treatment is provided on a fee-for-service basis.

If this medical insurance situation makes you uneasy, or if you do not have adequate medical insurance, then consider purchasing travelers' health insurance through a reputable travel agency or insurance company. Many plans are available, some of which can be combined with coverage for lost baggage, travel delays, and other vacation disasters. If you travel often, consider an annual travel insurance policy.

What to do if you have a non-life-threatening medical problem in London? Maybe a child comes down with an ear infection? Here are some medical resources for visitors:

- A few private walk-in medical clinics cater to tourists. For example, MediCentres are located in Victoria rail station and near the Bank Underground station, and there is a Medical Express Clinic on Harley Street.
- Call the front desk of your hotel. Most large hotels have on-call physicians or arrangements with medical centers, but these services can be expensive.
- The National Health Service operates walk-in centers, minor injury units, and hospital accident/emergency departments.
- In an emergency, telephone 999 for ambulance services.

One tactic used by traveling families is to pack a fairly extensive medical kit for overseas travel. Sometimes just carrying this kit acts like a talisman to keep illness at bay. Look up the generic names of any prescription medications, because brand names may be different outside your home country. In Britain, prescriptions are filled by chemists.

Money Matters—*Boy, Does It!*

For inside his hat was not just one, but a whole pile of coins. There were so many, in fact, that the latest addition— whatever it had been—was lost for all time amongst a vast assortment of pennies, three penny pieces, sixpences; coins of so many different shapes, sizes and values that Paddington soon gave up trying to count them all.

—*Paddington Goes to Town* by Michael Bond

The basic unit of currency in Britain is the pound. A pound (£) is divided into 100 pence (p). Here are common British currency denominations:

- Bills—£5, £10, £20, £50
- Coins—1 pence, 2 pence, 5 pence, 10 pence, 20 pence, 50 pence, £1, £2

For many years, Britain operated a complex, non decimal system

of currency. Although that old system is long gone, a tourist can still get confused, because the pound may occasionally be called a quid or even a bob.

Fumbling with unfamiliar bills and coins can ruin your image as a savvy tourist, so become familiar with the look and feel of pounds and pence before you start spending them. Learning about British coins can be an educational game, so try to obtain some coins before the trip and let children play with them.

Foreign currency looks so different that sometimes spending it hardly seems real. We call this the Monopoly money syndrome. But to avoid going bankrupt make a mental conversion to your home currency when spending pounds.

Whack-a-Mole Currency Rip-Offs

If there is one lesson to be learned about money and overseas travel, it is this: many banks, credit card companies, debit card issuers, and airport money exchanges are out to rip you off. They do this by imposing fees—sometimes deliberately hidden fees—on foreign currency transactions. Here are a few lies and half-truths that banks and others try to foist on travelers:

- If a local bank says, "We can get British pounds for you, in any amount, with no fees," it's forgetting to tell you, "But our exchange rate is about six percent higher than the rate at a British ATM."
- If a credit card company says, "The card is good at thousands of places in the UK," it's forgetting to add, "For a fee of four percent on each purchase."
- And if your otherwise trustworthy local travel agency offers to sell you a convenient tip pack in British pounds, be aware the markup can be outrageous.

Dynamic Currency Conversion

But wait, there's more. Let's say you use a credit card to pay a London hotel bill. The hotel may offer to conveniently charge your card in your home country's currency instead of pounds. Or sometimes they don't offer a choice and automatically process the transaction. This is dynamic currency conversion. It may seem like a good deal, but when the hotel charged your card in your home currency, it added a currency conversion fee. Worse, because the transaction is considered foreign, your credit card company may add its own fee. Bottom line—decline the offer and have the transaction processed in British pounds.

With all these potential traps, what can a traveler do? Read on for some hints, but keep in mind that today's best advice could easily change as new fees are imposed.

ATMs

If you normally use automatic teller machines to get cash, there is no reason to stop using ATMs when traveling to London. ATMs are also known as *cash points* in Britain. Here are some hints about using ATMs in London:

- Before traveling, check with your bank to make sure that your ATM card and personal identification number will work overseas.

- Many foreign ATMs allow access to checking accounts only, so do not count on being able to transfer funds between savings and checking using an overseas ATM.
- Convenience is a good reason to use ATMs, but there is another bonus. ATMs usually offer the best currency exchange rates.
- Be sure to use fee-free ATMs in London. ATMs associated with major British banks do not normally charge a user fee. But machines in pubs, convenience stores, and other areas may impose a fee or offer poor exchange rates.
- At the airport, be leery of ATMs operated by currency exchange companies and even some that seem to be bank affiliated. They do not offer the best rates.
- Your own bank may charge fees for each ATM transaction in London. In fact, some banks charge a foreign conversion fee *and* a foreign usage fee. So it pays to get an ATM/debit card with no fees.
- Some bank ATMs use optional dynamic currency conversion. If the ATM offers to process a cash withdrawal in your home currency, decline this option.

Credit Cards

Plastic is just as fantastic in London as it is at home. VISA and MasterCard are widely accepted in the UK, and credit card transactions are generally converted from pounds to your local currency at favorable exchange rates.

VISA and MasterCard International corporations add a small percentage fee for all foreign transactions. There is no escaping this fee. But the credit card issuer—the bank or credit union that issued the card—can add another, larger overseas transaction fee. Check with your bank and if it has this fee, find another credit card that does not.

We warned earlier about dynamic currency conversion. To avoid this, refuse to sign any credit card receipt that is not charged in the local currency. Just hand it back and say "Charge it in pounds." Some merchants may plead ignorance or claim that their credit card systems automatically charge the purchase in your home currency. That's not cricket, so play hardball here. In a pinch, sign the receipt and write on it "Merchant refused to charge in local currency." Then dispute the dynamic currency conversion charge through your credit card company.

Chip and PIN

In Britain, credit card users insert their cards into the front of a card reader and then enter a personal identification number into a keypad. This is the chip-and-PIN system. While many US credit cards come with embedded chips, most do not use a PIN number and still require a signature. Others cards still use magnetic strips. If you don't have a chip-and-PIN card, you might encounter occasional problems using credit cards in London, especially at unmanned locations like gasoline pumps and train station ticket machines.

Don't Leave Home Without It

Before leaving home, contact the your credit card companies and ATM card issuers to inform them that you will be traveling overseas. The reason? Credit card companies and banks monitor transactions. If these go from Wal-Mart $13.99, the Gap $29.95 . . . to Harrods £24.01, Fortnum & Mason £50.49, it may look like someone has stolen the card and gone on a London shopping spree. The card company may block further transactions. A blocked credit/ATM card overseas is a travel hassle to avoid.

Dash Cash

You have spent long hours on a plane, claimed luggage, cleared immigration and customs, and are navigating through an unfamiliar airport. The last thing you want to do is immediately search for a place to get British pounds. One way to avoid this hassle is to take a small amount of British currency on your trip—enough to buy a snack or cover a taxi ride to your hotel. Some travel agencies and banks sell foreign currency, and currency can also be purchased online. As noted previously, this is an expensive way to obtain pounds, but it is convenient.

That Nasty VAT

Many US residents are used to paying sales tax when they shop and readily accept a five or ten percent tax added to the sticker price. But in London, you're paying twenty percent in value-added tax (VAT) when you rent a hotel room, buy a gift, eat dinner, or rent a car.

Most quoted prices in Britain include the VAT. That is one reason some things look really expensive in London. The other reason is that many things *are* really expensive. Refunds of the VAT are possible on some purchases, but you have to spend a lot in one store, complete some paperwork, and go through an extra customs process at the airport when you depart. If you go into a London store and make a sizable purchase, the store may help process the VAT refund paperwork. Many people don't bother with it, especially if they are not buying a lot of merchandise. Unless you are a specially registered business traveler, you cannot recover the VAT on hotels, meals, or car rental. For tourists, this part of the VAT is an unavoidable cost of traveling.

Britspeak

England and America are two countries
separated by a common language.

—Attributed to George Bernard Shaw

For American visitors, one great thing about going to England is that the people speak our language...almost. There is no such thing as universal English. Many British words and phrases differ significantly from those used by Americans, Canadians, Australians, and other English-speakers. Then there is the issue of accents, even when words or phrases are the same.

Skip to the Loo

The wise parent of young children is always toilet aware. Families traveling to London should know from the start that "bathrooms" in Britain are rooms where you take a bath. If that's not what you're looking for, here are some of the British terms that do apply:

- Loo
- WC
- Lavatory
- Gents
- Ladies
- Nappy-changing room (for babies)
- Toilet (can't argue that)

Finding a public toilet is not too difficult in London. Locating a *free* toilet is a different matter. Toilets are available in many restaurants, hotel lobbies, museums, and larger retail stores. If you look respectable, usually no one objects if you use these facilities, and they are often cleaner than public toilets.

More Britspeak

We use the term *Britspeak* to refer to differences between American English and the language spoken by most of the inhabitants of London. Here are a few Britspeak definitions for US visitors:

Aubergine—Eggplant
Bill—Restaurant check
Biscuits—Cookies
Cash point—Automated teller machine
Chemist shop—Drugstore, pharmacy
Chips—French fries
Clotted cream—A thick, sweet cream used as a teatime spread for bread or scones
Coach—Bus
Crisps—Potato chips
Cuppa—Cup of tea
En suite—Private bath in a hotel room
First floor—Second floor
Flat—Apartment
Football—Soccer
Fortnight—Two weeks
Give way—Yield
Ground floor—First floor
Iced lolly—Popsicle
Lift—Elevator
Lorry—Truck
Nappy—Diaper
Petrol—Gasoline, expensive gasoline
Postbox—Mailbox
Pudding—Dessert (although dessert is also used)
Pushchair—Baby stroller
Queue—Line at a store, theater, or bus stop. Standing in queues is a national pastime in Britain.

Quid—A pound (£)
Roundabout—Traffic circle
Scheme—Plan or program (scheme does not have a negative connotation)
Scone—A pastry on which you pile clotted cream and jam at teatime.
Serviette—Napkin
Sterling—British pounds, money
Subway—Pedestrian underpass tunnel
Surgery—A doctor's or dentist's office
Takeaway—Carryout food
Tube—Subway
Underground—Subway
Way out—Exit
Zebra crossing—Pedestrian crossing (except at the zoo)

Tick-Tock

Although the clock face of Big Ben shows the familiar twelve hours, Britain officially uses a twenty-four-hour time system. Officially does not mean uniformly, and Londoners are more likely to say 3:00 p.m. than 1500. Deciphering morning hours is easy: 08:00 is 8:00 a.m., 10:00 is 10:00 a.m., and so forth. When confronted with unfamiliar afternoon times, just remember to subtract 1200. So 15:00 minus 12:00 equals 3:00 p.m. Colloquially, British people use the modifier "half" to mean half-past the hour. Thus "half-seven" means 7:30.

Time to Leave

No matter how long and fascinating your visit to London, eventually it will be time to leave. How do you know for sure? If you're a savvy tourist, one who tries to blend in with the local scene, it may be time to depart when other tourists ask you for directions.

Standing on a footbridge in St. James's Park, we were approached by an American tourist with an unmistakable regional accent.

"What's that building over there?" he asked.

"Buckingham Palace," we replied.

"Oh REALLY?" he answered, gawking in surprise.

Yes, it is definitely time to leave when other tourists mistake you for a local.

Back in the United States after fifteen days in London, our family unloaded piles of dirty laundry and then sat down to our first meal since returning home. Our son remarked, "I can't believe it. Last night we were having dinner at a pub in London. Today we're back at our kitchen table." That, son, is the magic of overseas travel. And it's the reason why we'll go back.

Photo Credits

pg. 6: photo © User:Colin/Wikimedia Commons. Creative Commons License (BY-SA 4.0). Jubilee_and_Munin,_Ravens,_Tower_of_London_2016-04-30.jpg

pg. 13 photo © Lily/lilivanili. Creative Commons License BY 2.0. ww.flickr.com/photos/lilivanili/5713228973

pg. 14 With permission of Royal Collection Trust © Her Majesty Queen Elizabeth II. Photographer: Derry Moore

pg. 19 photo by Kim Traynor. Creative Commons BY-SA 3.0 License, Via Wikimedia Commons

pg. 22 photo courtesy Westminster Abbey. © Jim Dyson/Westminster Abbey photo

pg. 25 photo by Aiwok (Own work). Creative Commons BY-SA 3.0 License, Via Wikimedia Commons

pg. 33, 34 photos courtesy Benjamin Franklin House. © Benjamin Franklin House

pg. 40 photo courtesy Imperial War Museum. © Imperial War Museum

pg. 43 photo courtesy Florence Nightingale Museum. © Florence Nightingale Museum

pg. 45 photo courtesy VisitLondon. © VisitLondon

pg. 52 photo courtesy VisitBritain. ©VisitBritain/Britain on View

pg. 53 photo courtesy Museum of London. ©Museum of London

pg. 55 photo courtesy VisitBritain. ©VisitBritain

pr. 57 photo courtesy VisitBritain. ©VisitBritain/Britain on View

pg. 58, 59 photos courtesy The Postal Museum. © The Postal Museum

pg. 66 photo courtesy VisitBritain. © Mikael Buck/Shrek's Adventure London

pg. 76, 78 photos courtesy The Royal Parks

pg. 79, 82 photos courtesy VisitLondon. © Pawel Libera/London and Partners

pg. 85 photo by Ian Wright. Creative Commons BY-SA 2.0 License. Via Wikimedia Commons

pg. 87 photo courtesy VisitBritain. ©VisitBritain/London Duck Tours

pg. 94 photo courtesy St Martin-in-the-Fields © St Martin-in-the-Fields

pg. 95 photo courtesy VisitBritain. ©VisitBritain/Britain on View

pg. 97 photo courtesy VisitBritain. ©British Tourist Authority

pg. 98 photo courtesy Kidzania. © Kidzania.

pg. 102 photo courtesy VisitBritain. ©VisitBritain/Pawel Libera

pg. 103 photo courtesy VisitBritain. ©VisitBritain/Simon Winnall

pg. 108 photo courtesy VisitBritain. ©VisitBritain/Jack Barnes

pg. 113 photo courtesy the London Zoo. © ZSL

pg. 114 photo courtesy SEA LIFE London Aquarium. © SEA LIFE London Aquarium

pg. 118, 118 photos courtesy VisitBritain. © British Tourist Authority

pg. 121 photo courtesy VisitBritain. © VisitBritain
pg. 130 photo courtesy VisitBritain. © British Tourist Authority
pg. 131 photo courtesy VisitBritain. © VisitBritain/Pawel Libera
pg. 134 photo courtesy and © London Museum of Water and Steam
pg. 137 photo © Jim Barton. Creative Commons License (CC BY-SA) via GeoGraph069
pg. 146 photo courtesy courtesy Legoland Windsor. © Lego
pg. 147 photo courtesy VisitBritain. © VisitBritain/Martin Brent Guest
pg. 149 photo courtesy VisitBritain. ©VisitBritain/Blenheim Palace
pg. 150 photos courtesy Blenheim Palace. © Blenheim Palace
pg. 152 photo by Monika. Creative Commons License CC BY-SA 2.0. Via www.flickr.com/
photos/17989497@N00/13952565657
pg. 154 photo courtesy © Anne Small
pg. 168 photo courtesy VisitBritain. © British Tourist Authority/Flackley Ash Hotel
pg. 172 photo courtesy VisitBritain. © VisitBritain/Kois Miah
pg. 173 photo courtesy and © Hyde Park Winter Wonderland /PWR Events/Simon
Derville
pg. 175 photo courtesy and © The Ritz Hotel London
pg. 176 photo courtesy and © IHG Group
pg. 178 photo courtesy and © Hilton Hotels and Resorts
pg. 179 photo courtesy and © St. Ermin's Hotel
pg. 180 photo courtesy and © The Stafford Hotel
pg. 184 photo courtesy and © Visit England
pg. 188 photo courtesy and © VisitBritain/Chesterfield Mayfair Hotel
pg. 193 photo courtesy and © VisitBritain
pg. 197 photo courtesy and © The National Trust
pg. 198 photo courtesy and © Historic Royal Palaces
pg. 203 photo courtesy and © British Airways
pg. 217 photo courtesy and ©Kidzania

Public domain photographs:
Front cover, pgs. vii, 4, 24, 28, 35, 47, 62, 117, 124, 133, 159, 187, 208, 210, 221

All other photographs © David Stewart White

About the Authors

David Stewart White began his adventures in family travel as a child, when he lived in Paris and traveled throughout Europe. His travel articles have appeared in the Washington Post, the Charlotte Observer, AAA World Magazine and in numerous travel websites and online magazines.

Deb Hosey White is the author of the novels *Pink Slips and Parting Gifts* and *Magic Numbers—The Actuary's Diary*. Her articles have appeared in the Washington Post, O.Henry magazine and The Three Tomatoes ezine. With English ancestors on both sides of her family, Deb is a serious Anglophile and an avid traveler.

In addition to the sixth edition of *Let's Take the Kids to London*, David and Deb are coauthors of *Portugal: A Tale of Small Cities*. Their Scotland guidebook is *Travels Beyond Outlander*. They also created *Beyond Downton Abbey* and *Travels Beyond Downtown*, a guidebook series exploring great British houses with fascinating stories.

Deb and Dave live and write in North Carolina, where they are partners in Scuppernong Books, an independent bookstore.

Index

T

U

V

W

Y

Z